Understanding Soc
An Empirical Ap

Understanding Social Work

An Empirical Approach

EILEEN MUNRO

THE ATHLONE PRESS
London & Atlantic Highlands, NJ

First published 1998 by
THE ATHLONE PRESS
1 Park Drive, London NW11 7SG
and 165 First Avenue,
Atlantic Highlands, NJ 07716

© Eileen Munro 1998

The right of Eileen Munro to be identified as the author of this work
has been asserted by her in accordance with the Copyright, Designs
and Patents Act 1988

British Library Cataloguing in Publication Data
*A Catalogue record for this book is available
from the British Library*

ISBN 0 485 11521 2 hb
0 485 12134 4 pb

Library of Congress Cataloging-in-Publication Data

Munro, Eileen, 1950–
    Understanding empirical social work / by Eileen Munro.
        p.   cm.
    Includes bibliographical references and index.
    ISBN 0-485-11521-2.—ISBN 0-485-12134-4 (pbk.)
    1. Social service—United States—Philosophy. 2. Social service—
United States—Methodology. 3. Social service—Research—United
States. I. Title.
    HV40.8.U6M85   1998
    361.3′2′0973 – dc21   97–31598
                                                                       CIP

Typeset by Ensystems, Saffron Walden

Printed and bound in Great Britain by
Bookcraft (Bath) Ltd

To the memory of my mother and father

Contents

Introduction

When I became a social worker, I was struck by the different ways we have of understanding clients and their problems. A young mother struggling to cope can be understood in two ways. She arouses feelings of empathy: we can sense her depression, loneliness and anxiety. Through talking to her and drawing on our own life experience, we can acquire a vivid understanding of her emotions and thoughts. At the same time, by using theories taught in training courses, we can explain her predicament in terms of social and economic factors, or relate it to her childhood experiences. These different ways of understanding human beings, empathic understanding and causal explanations, have created a perennial problem for social workers. Puzzlement about how to reconcile them in practice led me to study the philosophy of science and, in turn, to write this book.

Our ordinary skills in understanding ourselves and the people around us are built up over a lifetime, using our powers of empathy and intuitive reasoning. We acquire ideas about how and why people behave the way they do but this wisdom, though substantial, is, on the whole, implicit not clearly formulated. In contrast, theories in the social sciences are formally written out and publicly accessible. But these theories offer a more remote and intellectual kind of understanding. They tell us about causal factors but do not tell us how it feels to be subject to those influences.

Most social workers have thought that both sources of understanding have a valuable contribution to make to social work. The profession turned to the social sciences, at the beginning of this century, in the hope of strengthening its knowledge base, of developing a greater understanding of human problems and more effective ways of solving them. Commonsense wisdom has continued to seem indispensable in developing a helping relationship with clients. Formal theories and therapies cannot wholly replace the subtle and complex skills of communication acquired over years of experience.

Formal knowledge and intuitive understanding have not, however, been easy to reconcile. There have been long-standing debates about how to integrate theory and practice, to use heart and head, and to combine clear, logical reasoning with a caring and humane style. These problems are crucially dependent on what being scientific is thought to entail. The dominant scientific model, until recently, has been a behavioural/positivist one which, to many, has seemed irreconcilable with their existing wisdom. It seems not to build on social workers' intuitive and empathic understanding but to reject it as worthless and to demand a fundamentally different approach to studying clients. The rigorous calls from the scientific lobby for problems and goals to be described in terms of behaviour leaves social workers unclear about what place there is for their concern with clients' feelings, hopes and thoughts. Some, indeed, conclude that all scientists shares the extreme behaviourist John Watson's view that science has no interest in studying the mind. Science stresses the need for objectivity and social workers are left with an uneasy feeling that their aim of developing a close, helping relationship with clients is intrinsically at odds with a scientific approach. Consequently, scientific models have been unpopular in social work. Most see science as an enemy not an ally of their personal and caring approach to helping clients. The warmth and vividness of empathy contrasts with the cold logic of formal scientific theories. Many have concluded that a warm heart and a cool head do not go together. There is a widespread belief, as an American academic puts it: 'that reason and caring are incompatible' (Gambrill, 1990, p. 360).

For the majority, the conflict of heart and head is resolved in favour of the heart. They place the relationship first, valuing their personal skills of empathy and intuition above theories from the social sciences. Formal theories are not rejected but absorbed in a piecemeal way into their background knowledge where they inform the social worker's intuitive understanding but often in an unconscious way. In this tradition, social workers develop practice wisdom, a personal body of ideas based on their experience with clients as well as their social science training.

This private and individual style of social work has always presented problems in social work. It makes it difficult for practitioners to share their thinking, for others to judge it, and for the profession to build up a common body of knowledge.

But the problems it creates have become particularly acute today. Social work is under attack. After a century of expansion, in which social workers have been given a growing range of legal responsibilities and powers, their expertise is now being questioned. A series of well-publicised tragedies and scandals has made the general public aware of the power social workers have and how destructive it can be when used badly. Evaluative research has raised doubts about the quality of services many clients are receiving. Local authority management, under severe financial constraints, is wanting proof of value for money.

All of the critics are demanding evidence of what social workers are doing and reassurance that it is useful. Few doubt the good intentions of social workers but wanting to help clients, unfortunately, does not guarantee effectiveness. Social workers used to a personal, private way of working find it very hard to respond to demands to explain and justify themselves.

The social work profession is having to review its ways of reasoning and working. In recent years, there have been a wealth of articles in British and American journals on the nature of social work knowledge and research methods. The revival of the debate about social work knowledge is timely, however, not just because of pressures within social work but because major developments in our understanding of science have altered the premises of the art/science debate.

The Scientific Revolution in the seventeenth century had a profound effect on the Western World's view of nature. Religion was replaced by Reason in efforts to understand the universe and mankind's place in it. There was growing confidence that, by using human skills of rationality, people could understand, predict and control the natural and social worlds. The successes of science endorsed this confidence but those very successes also led scientists and philosophers to realise that there were fundamental flaws in the, previously dominant, positivist view of scientific method. The implications of these flaws have been widely debated. At one extreme, postmodernists argue that they show that the entire 'modernist' enterprise was misguided and that science is just one belief system among many with no justifiable claims to producing more reliable information than any other. This 'relativist' view of knowledge will be examined in Chapter

Eight. The main argument of this book, however, is that, far from undermining science, the revised empirical philosophies of science strengthen the case for a scientific approach to social work. They offer an account of scientific methods that can build on traditional social work methods instead of conflicting with them. Science *does* offer a way of meeting the growing demands for openness and accountability and social work hostility is based on a now obsolete image. There is a growing empirical practice movement in social work based on these new philosophies. It is not asking social workers to reject their empathic skills and intuitive wisdom but to be more rigorous and critical in using them. It is not just urging social workers to give more weight to the results of empirical studies but also encourages social workers to use the same standards of reasoning as researchers in their everyday practice. Recent books on research (e.g. Everitt, Hardiker, Littlewood, and Mullender, 1992; Fuller and Petch, 1995; Reid and Smith, 1989) offer a radically different approach from their positivist/behavioural forerunners (e.g. Tripodi, 1983).

A wider acceptance of this empirical approach is hampered by misunderstandings of how it differs from earlier models of scientific social work. This book describes the changes in our understanding of scientific methods and explains their practical significance. It emphasises the links between practice wisdom and scientific knowledge and demonstrates how science need not replace empathy and intuition but can provide ways of developing and checking them.

At first glance, social workers may think a book on philosophy is irrelevant to their problems. Philosophical discussions can seem esoteric and remote from the daily world of practice, a luxury, perhaps, to be enjoyed only by a few, underemployed academics. All social workers, however, base their practice on philosophical assumptions whether they are aware of them or not. These assumptions have a practical impact on the service the client receives. In assessing the risk of child abuse, for example, social workers have to decide what evidence is relevant, how reliable it is, and how they can use it to make a prediction about the safety of a particular child. The social worker who relies mainly on empathic and intuitive reasoning will use different evidence and methods of reasoning than a more scientific colleague and, in many cases, they will reach different decisions with considerable effect on the family concerned.

A discipline usually pays little attention to its philosophical foundations while the edifice it supports looks firm. It is typically in times of trouble, as now in social work, that the foundations come in for scrutiny. The picture in social work, however, is optimistic. There is a need to look at basic assumptions about practice but there is a viable alternative available that offers a constructive and exciting new model.

CHAPTER 1

The Need for Change

Social work needs to change in order to improve its service to clients and to silence its critics. Attacks come from many sources: from the general public and politicians, from senior management wanting to monitor practice more closely, and from critics within the profession concerned about the quality of help clients are receiving. Social workers are vulnerable when faced with demands for accountability because of the strong tradition of private, intuitive ways of working.

AUTONOMY AND ACCOUNTABILITY

Social workers have, until recently, retained a strong element of autonomy in their direct work with clients. The law may prescribe a responsibility, for example, for local authorities to 'promote the welfare of children' but it says little about how that responsibility is to be carried out. Management, in turn, sets limits on the resources and priorities of fieldworkers but the individual social worker has had considerable freedom in practice. The Department of Health and Social Security, reviewing studies of fieldwork, concluded that:

There is no way of knowing, from present research, what affects the choice of strategy adopted for particular clients, but it does appear to be left largely to the discretion of individual social workers. (1981, p. 65)

Parsloe and Stevenson in their extensive study of 31 social service teams reported a similar finding:

a feature of all the studies was the wide ranging freedom which social workers had to choose the style and content of their direct work with clients. (1978, p. 134)

McDonald's more recent research suggests no significant change in the intervening years. In a study of probation officers' report-writing and methods of intervention, she reports how probation officers differ in how they explain offenders' behaviour and in the methods of help they use: 'producing a picture of a professional or personal preference-led service, strongly influenced by ideological positions' (1994, p. 420).

The private nature of social work practice is increased because many practitioners have difficulty in explaining what they are doing. Several studies have found that social workers find it hard to describe their style of work, give their reasons for their choices, or formulate clear plans.

Goldberg and Warburton (1979) ran into this problem when they were trying to develop a record and review system to be used in local authority social services departments. Their aim was to collect standardised information on clients, the problems being tackled, and the methods and goals of the social workers. The researchers began by discussing some cases, chosen more or less at random, with each of the twenty social workers participating in the study. They hoped to get some general ideas on how the workers saw their jobs in order to form the basis of a recording system. They reviewed 113 cases in this way but found that the fieldworkers had great difficulty in describing either their goals or how they hoped to achieve them. Aims were expressed in indeterminate terms such as 'improving social functioning'. When asked their plans, most social workers described the client's present circumstances and difficulties but could not specify what they themselves planned to do to help them.

Parsloe and Stevenson met the same difficulties in their extensive study of 31 social services teams:

> several social workers indicated that they were unaccustomed to conceptualising or reflecting upon their practice. (1978, p. 135)

They concluded that social workers did not, in general, adopt a clearly thought-out approach:

> There was some evidence that many of the experienced workers were accustomed to working mainly on the intuitive level – in the sense of responding to the immediate situation without conscious reliance on a theoretical framework. (1978, p. 135)

Besides being unable to provide a clear account of their work to researchers, social workers also appear to run into trouble in explaining themselves to their clients. Mayer and Timms' famous study (1970) of clients' opinions of a Family Welfare Association service in London revealed widespread puzzlement about their social workers' aims and methods. The clients, in particular, did not understand their social workers' enthusiasm for talking while the social workers believed 'insight therapy' was their main technique. Sainsbury (1975) also found misunderstandings between clients and social workers about the purposes of social work involvement.

There is no evidence to suggest that these findings are now out of date. More recent research (Corby, 1982; Social Services Inspectorate, 1993) still reports social workers' problems in describing their plans or their methods.

But the days of seeing the social worker/client relationship as private are numbered.

Social workers are coming increasingly under scrutiny. The public have become more cautious about the degree of professional freedom social workers have. They have been concerned as a result of numerous scandals and tragedies. In some cases, social workers were failing to exercise their powers and take children away from dangerous parents. The horrific deaths of children like Maria Colwell (HMSO, 1974), Jasmine Beckford (London Borough of Brent, 1985), and Leanne White (Nottinghamshire Area Child Protection Committee, 1994), killed by their parents despite the activities of the caring professions, raised questions about professionals' competence and ability to deal with social problems. In other scandals, the fear was that social workers were using their powers too readily. The Cleveland and Orkney dramas, where many children were whisked away from their parents on apparently inadequate evidence of sexual abuse, made many worry about the degree of power society had handed over to social workers. The Staffordshire pindown controversy (Levy and Kahan, 1991) roused concern about the quality of care provided when children are taken away from home, a concern that has been greatly magnified by revelations about the extent of child sexual abuse in some residential homes (Clwyd Report, 1996). Research on the outcome for children in residential care has fuelled this worry (Social Services Inspectorate, 1991).

In the past 20 years, there have been 45 public inquiries into child abuse cases. These have produced recurrent criticisms, many of which echo research findings about the dominant style of social work practice (Munro, 1996 and 1997). Social workers' failure to be clear and explicit about their plans, reasons, and methods are a persistent refrain throughout these reports. The practitioners were faulted for poor or non-existent recording, leaving supervisors and subsequent workers in ignorance of what had been going on. In many cases, unclear plans led to misunderstandings and omissions in collaborating with other professionals. Woolly plans also created problems in evaluating progress. The picture of good practice that emerges from these reports is that clear, explicit assessments, plans and reviews are essential to minimise the risk of errors. This is far removed from the typical intuitive and personal approach favoured by most social workers and portrayed in the inquiry reports.

Extensive guidelines and procedures have now been introduced into child protection work, reducing social workers' range of autonomy and encouraging a move towards a more open and critical form of practice. Studies by the Social Services Inspectorate of six local authority departments, however, show that social workers are slow to change. 'Inspectors seldom found comprehensive assessments . . . information was not collated, analyzed or used to form a plan' (SSI, 1993, p. 28). All were failing to 'formulate child protection plans' (1993, p. 29). The quality of record-keeping was so poor that 'this was an aspect of performance requiring urgent attention' (1993, p. 33).

Changing political views on economic and political theories are also producing change in social work. The Conservative government saw the welfare state as a burden on the wealth-producing sector of the economy since funding social services requires high taxes. In debates reminiscent of the nineteenth century worries about the harmful effects of charity, politicians argue that the welfare system has encouraged dependency and discouraged self-help and family support. Recent social legislation is intended to counteract this tendency, stressing the importance of individual responsibility, choice and freedom. The paternalism of earlier legislation is replaced with the concept of partnership between state and client. The social worker should negotiate with and on behalf of the client to create a care plan, drawing on family, community and, if unavoidable, statutory sources of help. Clear, agreed plans and contracts are a key feature of this new style of work. The shift in the balance of power in favour of the client is a development welcomed by many whatever their political views.

Demands for clarity also come from clients. The new emphasis on partnership in community care and child care services entails more openness. Clients can only give informed consent to a care plan if they understand the options available and the choices being made.

The effects of this change in basic political philosophy filter down to direct social work in many forms. For example, the importance given to demonstrating value for money requires close scrutiny of social work practice so that managers are becoming far more involved in monitoring performance and, indirectly, in prescribing direct work with clients. Collecting information is central to monitoring and evaluating practice, requiring fieldworkers to write down what they are doing in more detail than ever before and to provide their seniors with statistics to enable them to cost and evaluate the workings of the department. As Parton points out:

An increasing emphasis is placed on the production of mission statements, objectives, outcomes, statistics, community care plans, and annual reviews. The management of information itself becomes the central rationale for policy and practice, from those in central government to professionals on the front line. (1994, p. 26)

But who determines what information to manage? Information is not a neutral material. The performance indicators selected create a picture of social work practice. Elements of practice that are not included are in danger of being ignored and undervalued. Therefore decisions on what information to gather are very influential and whoever makes those decisions has considerable power. One criterion in making them is a judgement about what aspects of social work practice are important for evaluating good practice. But some aspects are easier to measure than others and if priority is given to ease of collection when deciding on data then a distorted picture of social work will be created.

In monitoring, for example, a Section 47 investigation into an allegation of child abuse, the time taken to complete the investigation is one piece of information most managements collect. It is simple to record but without other details it is hard to judge its relevance. Speed is a desirable feature to some extent in order to minimise the stress on the family and it is encouraged in the Department of Health's (1991) guidelines. It is not however a simple indicator of good practice. An individual case might be dealt with swiftly because it proved to be quite simple and straightforward, the speed might be achieved by a cursory, inaccurate investigation, or it might result from a particularly competent worker handling the complexities of the case well. Similarly taking an unusually long time over an investigation might be due to heavy caseloads, inefficient staff, or a complex case needing considerable time and skill to be assessed. More information about the quality and content of the work is needed to make an informed judgement about the social work practice.

Social workers are vulnerable because of the long tradition of working in a private way. Valued aspects of practice, interviewing and relationship skills for instance, can be the hardest to articulate and describe in statistics. But however complicated the task, the demands of modern management for more information about practice are a compelling argument for trying to formulate the ideas considered important in providing a good social work service. There is evidence that decisions on how to monitor and evaluate practice are being made by senior management and imposed on practitioners (Hadley and Clough, 1996). This re-shaping of their work is causing anger and frustration but efforts to oppose it must recognise the need for public accountability. To be effective, resistance should be aimed not at the concept of performance indicators itself but at the inadequacey and insensitivity of the ones in current use.

DOUBTS ABOUT EFFECTIVENESS

There is no strong research tradition in social work so that, compared for instance with medicine, there are few studies testing the effectiveness of different social work methods of helping clients with particular problems. The research that has been done has a limited readership. Social work hostility or indifference to science is shown in their attitude to research. Yet training courses have always stressed the importance of looking to research for guidance on practice methods. The Central Council on Education and Training in Social Work asserts that 'social workers must be able to apply research findings to practice' (CCETSW, 1989, p. 11). But this aspect of training seems to have little impact. Studies in both America and Britain found that few social workers read research reports, used their results in practice, or rated research as helpful to them (Rosenblatt [1968], Kirk [1976], Davies [1974], Shaw and Walton [1978])

Research studies, however, have some important lessons for social workers though some of them make uncomfortable reading. It is useful to examine them in two groups: the large-scale controlled trials mainly carried out in the USA in the 1950s and 1960s, and the generally smaller studies conducted in both Britain and the USA in recent years.

The first wave of research started in the 1950s. It covered a wide range of social work client groups, for instance evaluating services for disturbed children, delinquents, ethnic minorities, low-income multi-problem families, frail elderly people, and families of alcoholics. It also covered a range of social work methods. The most common was individual casework based on psychoanalytic theories but, in most cases, workers also paid attention to clients' problems with their families, schools, and money. Group work, in a variety of forms, was studied. All the studies reviewed had a control group but in some cases this group received no service and in others it received a rival service so that the study compared, for example, trained and untrained workers.

The results were a shock to social workers. They are summed up by one reviewer, Joel Fischer:

Lack of effectiveness appears to be the rule rather than the exception across several categories of clients, problems, situations, and types of casework. (1973, p. 19)

People have tried to discredit the findings of these studies by claiming the research was done by opponents of social work who were wanting to prove it useless. This is not true. Social workers at the time wanted their work evaluated because they were confident it was effective and they wanted to demonstrate this to a wider audience. It may be hard for social workers today to appreciate the optimism of that time when economies were thriving and there was money and motivation to tackle the major social problems. Social work was expanding fast and, particularly in America where there was a high percentage of trained social workers, there was a strong belief in the power of practice methods based on psychoanalytic theories. Mullen and Dumpson who reviewed this research, describe the mood in which the research was conducted in America:

> Social work emerged from the 50s with confidence concerning its effectiveness. As a profession, it sought expanded opportunities and resources to demonstrate its competence. The 60s witnessed a marked increase in those opportunities, and social work set out to demonstrate its relevance. Out of this confidence social workers boldly exposed their practice to the critical scrutiny of scientific evaluation and assumed that such evaluations would assist them as they refined their technologies and expanded their knowledge. They assumed, too, that these evaluations would clearly demonstrate the effectiveness of their interventive efforts. (Mullen and Dumpson, 1972, p. 251)

Unfortunately, Mullen and Dumpson can only reach the same depressing conclusion as Joel Fischer:

> The researchers, for many reasons, were rarely able to conclude that a program had even modest success in achieving its major goals (p. 42.)

The results of these studies shook the confidence of social workers and they have been examined, analyzed, and debated by many authors – Segal (1972), Fischer (1973 and 1976), Wood (1978), and Sheldon (1986). While some have tried to put the point in a gentler manner, none has disagreed with the negative conclusions of Fischer and Mullen and Dumpson.

Besides learning that the services were not as effective as had been believed, there is a second, equally important, lesson to be learnt from these evaluations: social workers are poor judges of their own practice. Over many decades, American social workers developed and refined methods of working which they thought were highly effective but which, when compared with rival or no treatment, showed no superiority. Since personal judgement plays such a big part in current social work, this finding is at least as worrying as the evidence of the ineffectivessness of so many methods of working.

Many factors contribute to the unreliability of social workers' appraisal of their own practice. If they have put in a lot of effort, they will hope that their labours are successful. They therefore cannot look at the evidence in a neutral way and may be biassed in what they notice or how they interpret their observations.

This has been classically demonstrated in some inquiries into child abuse tragedies. Jasmine Beckford and her sister, for example, had been taken into care after suffering physical abuse from their father – Jasmine had a broken leg and her sister a broken arm. Her social worker put in an impressive quantity of work with the parents to improve their ability to cope with the tasks of parenting. She had formed a close relationship particularly with the mother and appreciated the strength of her desire to look after her own children. So, when the children went home on trial after eight months, the social worker wanted the rehabilitation to succeed. In the following two years, she noticed only the evidence of success. She failed to notice that Jasmine, who had gained weight and height dramatically while in a foster home, was steadily deteriorating physically; she did not query her long absences from nursery school, one of which, the inquiry found, coincided with a broken leg; she did not tell the school of Jasmine's history or ask them to monitor her so that when teachers saw injuries they did not think of the possibility of abuse; she believed everything the parents told her. The inquiry report describes her as 'naive almost beyond belief', saying that 'as soon as the social workers thought they saw the first signs of improved conduct on the part of Morris Beckford and Beverley Lorrington, an overweening optimism took hold' (London Borough of Brent, 1985, p. 127). Professor Greenland, explaining the social workers' blindness to what, with hindsight, looks so obvious, told the inquiry that 'the rule of optimism' was a powerful influence in child protection work:

> Because problems are so complex, in order to develop enough enthusiasm and enough energy, the social workers tend to have a very optimistic view of what can be accomplished. They tend to exaggerate progress that has been made, and they may see progress where there is no progress. (London Borough of Brent, 1985, p. 217)

Social workers' perception may be biassed but there may also be bias in the information they are given particularly by clients. In child protection work, parents have strong reasons for lying. It is not surprising that Jasmine Beckford's parents tried to hide Jasmine's injuries from the social worker since discovery would have led to losing the children and criminal proceedings. But clients may lie for less obvious reasons as well. One recurrent finding of research is that many clients appreciate the efforts of their social workers. Practitioners may not be effective but they try hard and clients are grateful to them so they can be reluctant to be critical and may offer a rosier picture of progress than is true.

The other major source of distortion in social workers' judgements of the effectiveness of their efforts is ignorance of the 'natural history' of the problem – of what would have happened if the client had received no help from the social worker. People have many other sources of assistance, including their own problem-solving skills, and time alone may be sufficient to alleviate some difficulties. This means that social workers may see improvement in their clients but it is hard to judge whether this is *because of* the social work help. Several critics in Fischer's (1976) review of the American research argue that the negative results cannot be true because they conflict with practitioners' personal experience. One of the critics, Werner, states categorically that he himself has observed 'that casework has been markedly effective with hundreds of clients.' Large numbers of his colleagues, he claims, have had a similar experience so that they are certain 'that many of their clients after casework services have become happier, less anxious, stronger, more successful, or more competent in problem-solving' (Fischer, 1976, p. 325). The problem is that the clients may well be markedly better, but they might have improved anyway without the worker's help. The controlled trial where clients receiving the service are compared with an untreated control group provides the strongest evidence on whether the treatment has had any specific effect on the course of the problem. When studies report that people without treatment showed the same improvements as those who received it, the claim that the treatment is effective is seriously undermined.

What has been the reaction of the social work profession to this depressing set of results? For many, the immediate reactions were to ignore them or dismiss them as invalid in some way. Some British social workers saw

them as irrelevant since they showed American not
British failure, though, since American social workers
generally have more training and more resources, this
seems a dubious defence. Many still pay no attention to
them; the research is not even mentioned on some
training courses. If anything, it appears to have increased
social workers' hostility to research generally. Its failure
to endorse practitioners' own optimistic assessments of
their work is taken by some to show that research, not
social workers' self-evaluation, is at fault.

An irrational, knee-jerk rejection of the results is more
understandable when you consider the size of the problem
social workers were facing. Their entire approach to social
work seemed to be undermined. But if none of their
familiar ways of working were effective, what were they
to do when faced with a client?

Scientists faced with results that falsify their theory
have three options: to reject the theory, to modify it so
that it can account for the results, or to show that the
results are inaccurate and therefore they, rather than the
theory, should be rejected. All these options were followed by different groups in social work.

Some have tried to undermine the accuracy of the
results or suggest ways of improving practice. They have,
however, been hampered by the nature of the studies.
The researchers had concentrated on *outcome*, paying
scant attention to the *process* of helping. There was little
detailed description of the social work service that had
been evaluated. We know that the studies ranged over
individual, family, and groupwork methods. In some
cases, social workers offered predominately a counselling
service; in others this was combined with practical help
and advice. But this degree of description is of very
limited value. Within each category, social workers may
vary a great deal in what they do. A psychoanalytic
approach using Freudian theory for example differs from

one based on Klein. This lack of detail made it hard for people questioning the results or suggesting changes to establish their case.

Strean (in Fischer, 1976) shows one attempt to question the relevance of the results. He argues that the negative results reflect social workers' incompetence in using psychoanalytic theories rather than casting doubt on the theories themselves: 'psychodynamic theory is poorly and fragmentally utilized, abused and misapplied by many if not most caseworkers in their practices.' If this argument were accepted, better training, not a change of theory, would be required. Another problem in interpreting the findings is posed by Fischer (1973) who argues that, on close analysis, the results of many studies suggest that some in the experimental group *deteriorated* more and others *improved* more than members of the control group but the *average* results for the two groups were the same and concealed this difference. It may be that the method was effective in skilled hands but positively harmful when used by incompetent practitioners. This argument, if true, would be very worrying and again more training would be recommended. Wood (1978) suggests that the practice evaluated might have been ineffective because it was of poor quality and she proposes certain principles of 'quality practice'. All of them are familiar and each, as she acknowledges, has long been a part of practice theory so it would be surprising if they had been ignored by all the social workers whose practice was evaluated.

The trouble is that without detailed information about the form and the quality of the social work service, these various arguments cannot be settled on the present evidence. Further research designed specifically to check these arguments is needed. But conducting such research is difficult when social workers themselves have trouble in being explicit about what they do. If research is to play a constructive role in helping social workers identify effective strategies while eliminating harmful or useless methods, then we need to study process as well as outcome.

Another option for scientists faced with falsifications is to reject the theory and many social workers have done this. The negative message of the research seems to have seeped into general awareness, leading to a perceptible drop in confidence in casework based on psychoanalytic theories. For Pearson, Treseder and Yellolly (1988) this a cause for concern, since they argue that social workers are losing a valuable source of understanding. The value of such understanding however is very dubious since not only has psychoanalytic casework failed to demonstrate its value, but studies of psychoanalytic therapies generally have produced poor results This conclusion has been reached by the well-known critic of psychoanalysis Hans Eyesenck (1986) and also by psychoanalysts themselves. Glover in a textbook on the subject, comments: 'I have included therapeutic efficacy in the list of unwarranted assumptions [about psychoanalysis]' (1955, p. 376). Another analyst Strupp concedes: 'in critically assessing the current status of psychoanalytic psychotherapy one cannot fail to record a certain disappointment with the achievements and promise of this method of therapy' (1968, p. 333). Indeed Pearson *et al* themselves admit that 'whenever psychoanalytical theory and therapy has been put to the test of experimental scrutiny, for example, it tends not to fare very well' (1988, p. 18).

In place of psychoanalysis, no single theoretical approach has gained dominance. As the following chapter will show, many social workers have no clear, explicit knowledge base to their practice.

But there have also been attempts to find a new theoretical foundation and to avoid the errors of the past when social workers believed mistakenly that they were being highly effective. This has led to the re-appraisal of a scientific approach and the growing interest in how scientific methods can be used by social workers. The empirical practice movement, as Reid (1994) calls it, encourages social workers to use empirically tested methods of helping, to formulate their reasoning, and to evaluate their own work rigorously. It is not restricted to a behavioural foundation but shares that discipline's concern with empirical testability.

The influence of the empirical movement is clearly seen in more recent studies of social work. Besides the different theoretical base, these studies have produced far more favourable results. In reviews of research done between 1973 and 1979 (Reid and Hanrahan, 1980) and between 1979 and 1991 (Macdonald and Sheldon, 1992) positive results far outweigh mixed or negative outcomes.

Reid and Hanrahan looked at evaluations of direct social work practice carried out in the United States and Canada between 1973 and 1979. They restricted their review to research with an experimental design where clients were randomly allocated to service or control groups. They found 18 studies meeting their criteria. In contrast to the earlier research, they found that 'all but two or three of the 18 studies yielded findings that could on balance be regarded as positive' (1980, p. 15). The other major difference between these studies and their predecessors was in the type of social work practice being evaluated. In Fischer's review, casework based on psychoanalytic theories had been the most common social work method studied. In these more recent ones:

one is struck by the dominance of structured forms of practice in these experiments – that is, of practice that takes the form of well-explicated, well-organised procedures usually carried out in a stepwise manner and designed to achieve relatively specific goals. The influence of the behavioural movement is quite apparent and pervasive (1980, p. 11).

Macdonald and Sheldon (1992) scanned British and American professional journals between January 1979 and January 1991 for reports of social work evaluations. They had more liberal criteria than Reid and Hanrahan, including not only studies using an experimental design but also client opinion research and what they called 'pre-experimental' studies which did not have a randomly created comparison group but generally measured change by comparing pre-test and post-test measurements. They found reports of 95 evaluative studies of social work. Most were conducted in the USA particularly those with the more rigorous experimental design, only 13 per cent of which were carried out in Britain.

The most interesting finding is that 75 per cent of them showed positive results. A broad range of social work problems were dealt with, including: family problems, child protection work, mental disorder, offenders, adoption and fostering practice, and services for the elderly. Unlike Reid and Hanrahan's review, they found a broad range of social work methods. Behavioural and cognitive-behavioural methods formed the largest group (31 studies). The next biggest group (26 studies) they gave the traditional name of 'casework' defining it as social work practice with the key features of: '(a) reliance upon an historical analysis (aetiological/developmental) of problems; (b) use of reflective questions and discussion to encourage the development of insight into the causes of these as the main vehicle of useful change; (c) attention also to social, financial and practical difficulties' (1992, p. 628). There were also 7 studies of family therapy and 11 studies of non-behavioural groupwork. The other 20 studies were grouped into an 'other' category, covering 'a scatter of therapeutic approaches such as crisis intervention ... and mediation between offenders and their victims' (1992, p. 629). Looking at the results in more detail, 70 per cent of the behavioural and cognitive/

behavioural studies produced positive results, as did 16 of the 26 'casework' studies, 6 of the 7 evaluations of family therapy, 6 of the 11 non-behavioural groupwork studies, and 12 of the 20 in the 'other' category. While the casework group of studies have the worst results, they are still considerably better than the results of the big trials of the 1950s and '60s.

These recent studies are very promising, suggesting that social workers can offer valuable help to their clients. But their findings need to be learnt and acted upon more widely in the profession before we shall see a widespread improvement in the standard of practice. So far, they have not aroused the interest one might have hoped among fieldworkers. The majority of social workers are consistent in ignoring positive as well as negative findings. This reflects the widespread belief that empirical/scientific methods of evaluation are not applicable to most forms of social work, that they are in some way unsuited to examining the subtle nuances of the helping relationship and can only produce crude and inaccurate results. With this belief, a healthy scepticism about empirical research looks reasonable. But it is based on a false picture of science. Many social workers continue to believe that, in the social sciences, science equals behaviourism. To them, the request to adopt more scientific ways of evaluating their work is a covert way of encouraging them to abandon their current ways of working and adopt a behavioural approach. This misunderstanding is not helped by the fact that so many of the recent studies are indeed of behavioural forms of therapy, though this is mainly due to the strong research tradition among behaviourists. Nor is it helped by the way that the most vocal commentators on the earlier negative research, Joel Fischer in the USA and Brian Sheldon in Britain, have since been urging behavioural approaches on their social work colleagues, though their advocacy is based on the impressive results of evaluative studies rather than any unique claims to being scientific.

This review of research in social work produces four central lessons. First, many forms of social work practice have been unable to demonstrate positive results when clients' progress is matched against a group of untreated people with similar problems. Secondly, this is despite practitioners believing strongly that they were being very effective; their own appraisals of their work seem unreliable. A third lesson is that unless research studies the process as well as the outcome of social work help, results are difficult to use to improve expertise. The final lesson is that social workers' indifference or outright hostility to empirical research has far-reaching implications. Studies cast doubt on the efficacy of many popular methods of working while suggesting more fruitful approaches which social workers find less attractive. If doctors allowed personal taste and questions of 'style' to determine what drugs they gave patients, ignoring the evidence from clinical trials, there would be public outcry and patients would sue them for malpractice. Although there are differences between studying the impact of a chemical on the body and the effect of psycho-social help on a client, they do not make the results reliable in one case and useless in the other. Reluctance to take research results as accurate is part of the widespread anti-science views in social work. The need to take the lessons of research seriously provides another reason for questioning this rejection of science.

CONCLUSION

Traditionally, the key feature of social work help has been the relationship with the client. Understanding and offering assistance to clients has been mediated through the social worker's private skills in relating. To most social workers, the helping relationship has seemed central to effective practice and also in direct conflict with a scientific approach. Although drawing on theories from the social sciences, most develop a personal and private style of working, relying on their own appraisal of their work and ignoring as irrelevant the findings of empirical research.

In recent years the private nature of social work practice has been increasingly challenged. Much-publicised tragedies and scandals have aroused worries among the general public about social workers' competence and the extent of their power. The shift in political and economic thinking has produced new demands for accountability. To act as 'partners' in their care, clients need to understand what help social workers can give. Senior managers who have to justify expenditure and ensure they are meeting statutory requirements also need to know the details of social workers' practice.

Traditional social work practice is also under attack from research evidence, casting doubt on the effectiveness of many practice methods, and on social workers' ability to judge their own work. Recent research is also producing evidence suggesting that more systematic and structured approaches may be of greater use to clients. Research highlights, too, the need to make social work methods explicit so that process as well as outcome can be studied. Without this, the practical value of empirical studies is severely limited in helping social workers to improve their practice.

Social work needs to change but can it do so without losing the elements of personal skill and concern for the client's feelings and thoughts which have been so valued? The dominant view in social work is that the skills of understanding and helping people are personal and private; they cannot be written out as formal theories which can be empirically tested. In the rest of this book, I shall defend the empirical practice movement, arguing that opponents have a false picture of science and it is possible for social workers to incorporate scientific methods into their current style of working. Moreover, social workers are being forced to articulate their work to some degree by new legal and management requirements. If they do not learn to make the valued but more nebulous aspects of their practice public, these will be overlooked by managers measuring cost-effectiveness and will not figure in contracts with clients. There is therefore a strong danger that they will be eradicated from social work.

CHAPTER 2

Social Workers' Role
and Expertise

Social work is not, in essence, a new activity although it has emerged over the past century as a new profession. People have always helped each other with personal and social problems. Religious organisations, the Poor Law system, and charities have provided more formal services. Modern professional social work is distinctive, however, in its claim to expertise and in the duties and powers it has been given by legislation. The two factors are entwined. The growing role of social work arises not only from society's concern about social problems but also from a belief that social workers have special skills in dealing with those problems. But what is the nature of their expertise?

This chapter starts by examining the way the profession has grown and details the tasks, the main statutory responsibilities and powers, that have been assigned to it. There has always been debate about what expertise is needed to carry out these duties. The history of social work training illustrates the increasing value given to theoretical knowledge drawn from the social sciences. There is debate about what theories should be taught. There is also controversy about the purpose of this formal training, about how theories are to be *used*. There is a long-standing problem about how to integrate theory into practice. The predominantly private style of working, discussed in the previous chapter, makes it difficult to say what expertise social workers are actually using in their direct work with clients though research studies provide some valuable evidence.

THE GROWTH OF THE SOCIAL WORK PROFESSION

Over the past two centuries, the State has become increasingly involved in welfare issues. Alongside the giants of education, health, income maintenance, and housing, social work has progressed from its birth in the slums of nineteenth century London, with a spurt in the post-war creation of the Welfare State, to its current standing as an important and costly public service. There is nothing new in trying to help people in trouble, but the distinctive feature of the past hundred years is the growing formalisation of helping services and the emergence of the professional social worker as a person with particular training and competence.

Although now seen as a single profession, social work's roots are in a variety of charitable services which developed to deal with a range of social problems.

The Society for Organising Charitable Relief and Repressing Mendicity (later re-named the Charity Organisation Society, COS) is a major ancestor, creating 'caseworkers', recognisable as predecessors of today's social workers. The COS was formed because of a growing fear that the numerous charities at the time were giving out aid indiscriminately and positively harming the poor by encouraging dependency instead of self-help. The caseworker's job was to interview applicants for alms and assess their needs, circumstances, and character. Most importantly, she had to judge the likely impact of giving help. Would it be beneficial, helping the person to return to self-sufficiency, or harmful, re-enforcing their laziness or depravity? The 'deserving' poor did not just get money but were also offered help in the form of a supportive relationship as they tried to tackle their problems. The 'undeserving' poor – 'persons of drunken, immoral, or idle habits' (COS 1890) were turned away with Poor Law Relief their only source of aid. The caseworker's concern for accurate diagnosis followed by treatment persists in the modern emphasis on a thorough assessment and planned intervention.

The origins of social work with the ill and disabled can be traced back to the first 'lady almoner', Mary Stewart, who was appointed at the Royal Free Hospital in London in 1895. The almoners' primary task was to check how much patients could afford to pay for medical treatment. In assessing the patients' circumstances and needs, they soon became interested in extending their role to dealing with the practical problems caused by illness and later with the social and psychological difficulties it created. Their financial task ended in 1948 when the National Health Service was created but almoning had by then established itself as a useful social service. In 1951 the Cope Report, reviewing the work of medical auxiliaries including almoning, judged that 'the work of the almoner should be regarded as one of the essential elements of a complete hospital service, and indeed of a complete health service' (1951, para. 115).

Nowadays, people who suffer from physical or mental illness or disability form the largest group of social work clients. Modern policies on care for people with all forms of illness and disability have shifted the emphasis from institutional to community care. The 1990 National Health Service and Community Care Act greatly increased the role of social services in the care of the ill and disabled, giving local authorities the prime responsibility for providing community care.

Two radically different branches of social work developed for people with mental illness. In the community, the primary task was to help in arranging compulsory admissions to hospital. The Receiving Officers of the Poor Law had a practical role in helping doctors and magistrates to certify people as lunatics and get them into asylums. While the magistrate's role in compulsory admissions has since disappeared, the Receiving Officer's part has gradually become more important and more clearly identified as the work of a skilled social worker. The 'Duly Authorised Officer' of the first half of this century was replaced in the 1959 Mental Health Act by the 'Mental Welfare Officer' who, in turn, was superseded in the 1983 Mental Health Act by the 'Approved Social Worker'. This latest Act also stipulates that ASWs should be trained before being appointed.

The hospital-based psychiatric social work service has an unusual history. Other social work specialisms developed as a social need was identified whereas psychiatric social work began when a new therapeutic approach was recognised. In the 1920s, American social workers, like many others, had been very impressed by the work of Sigmund Freud. Psychoanalytic theories seemed to offer both a compelling explanation of clients' emotional problems and a therapy for helping them. British observers were impressed by the American developments and the Commonwealth fund provided money to send some social workers to America to learn the new approach. These social workers subsequently set up the first university-based social work training course at the London School of Economics in 1929. Only after completing this training did the first psychiatric social workers start work in mental hospitals and child guidance clinics.

Children's welfare has long been a focus of charitable concern and is nowadays the area in which social workers get the most public attention and criticism. As statutory services were set up, the main emphasis of early child care workers was in providing alternative care for children whose parents were unable for any reason to look after them adequately. The Public Assistance Department of the local authority was responsible for children in care under the Poor Law while, after the Children and Young Persons Act 1933, the Education Department was responsible for children taken into care under that legislation. The division of responsibilities caused confusion and the 1948 Children Act established a single Child Care Department responsible for all the local authority's various duties.

Over the years, there has been growing appreciation of children's needs and rights and the limitations of substitute care. Nowadays, priority is given to helping the family to cope with any difficulties that arise with children being removed as infrequently and for as little time as possible. The most recent legislation, the Children Act 1989 (Section 17), recognises the value of children being brought up by their own parents if at all possible. It makes it a duty of the local authority to 'safeguard and promote the welfare of children within their area who are in need' and to 'promote the upbringing of such children by their families, by providing a range and level of services appropriate to those children's needs.' Allied to this change in policy, is a significant increase in the knowledge and skills social workers are expected to have in working with children and families both in assessing their needs and in helping them function better. The public inquiries into child abuse deaths show that the public have high expectations of social workers investigating and dealing with cases of child abuse.

The roots of the Probation Service are found in the nineteenth century practice of some magistrates who feared the corrupting effects of prison on young men, and preferred to release first-time offenders on the condition that they 'kept the peace'; sometimes they attached a condition of supervision by a parent or guardian. Organised supervision began in 1876 when the Church of England Temperance Society appointed a 'missionary' to some London police courts. The courts would release the convicted offender on the condition that he would see the missionary who would 'advise, assist, and befriend' him and help him lead an honest life. The success of this innovation led to the Probation and Offenders Act 1907 which enabled all magistrates courts to appoint probation officers. As in other branches of social work, their duties have subsequently mushroomed. They are still involved in supervising offenders on probation orders. They also help courts in their sentencing decisions by providing pre-sentence reports; they supervise offenders on Community Service Orders; they provide support to prisoners while in detention and after release, and have a significant role in divorce and custody proceedings, providing, court reports, marriage counselling, and conciliation services.

The re-organisation of the personal social services in 1968 in Scotland and 1970 in England and Wales is a major landmark in the expansion of social work, creating large local authority departments with political influence and uniting the various services into a single social work profession. By the 1960s, several forms of social work had become established in various local authority departments, the health service, and the criminal justice system. This arrangement was seen to lead to problems with duplication, poor co-ordination, and gaps in services. At the same time there was growing recognition of the similarity in the work of the various helping agencies, irrespective of their client group. Pressure grew for a re-organisation and integration of services. In Scotland, the Kilbrandon report (1964) reviewed the personal social services and recommended setting up Social Work

Departments which would have responsibility for all social work, including probation. The recommended changes were brought in by the Social Work (Scotland) Act 1968. The Seebohm Committee (1968), facing the same task in England and Wales, reached similar conclusions, recommending the setting up of Social Services Departments which would bring together: the child care service, the welfare services, education welfare and child guidance services, the home help service, mental health social work services, adult training centres, day nurseries, and the supervision of childminders. The proposals were implemented in the Local Authority Social Services Act (1970). Unlike the Scottish system, probation remained as a separate service. Medical and psychiatric social work stayed under hospital management until the local government re-organisation in 1974 transferred them to the local authorities.

This brief look at the history of social work reveals several important developments.

In the histories of each of the different branches of social work there has been a shift from the voluntary to the statutory sector. The Church of England Temperance Society funded the first court missionaries but the Home Office is now responsible for probation officers' salaries. The first lady almoner was paid by the Charity Organisation Society but her successors in hospital social work are employed by the local authority. The majority of social workers nowadays operate through local authority social services departments and the probation service. A substantial minority (estimated by Byrne and Padfield [1990, p. 403] as about a third) are still employed in voluntary welfare agencies such as the NSPCC and the Family Welfare Association, but even these are often linked, through funding, to the state provision of welfare.

The move to the statutory sector has led to social

workers acting within a legal framework of responsibilities and powers, unlike the early caseworkers of the COS who could choose who received their services. Laws have not only increased social workers' duties but also their powers. They play a significant role in many cases where people's civil liberties are removed. They may be involved in arranging a compulsory admission to a psychiatric hospital, or in removing children from their parents. Many people are placed by law in the care of or under the supervision of social workers. Besides those cases where social workers have overt authority, they also have extensive power over most apparently voluntary clients who often have no choice about receiving social work help since there is no alternative source of aid. Few parents of children with learning difficulties, for instance, are rich enough to buy all the social services they need in the private sector.

The history of the past hundred years demonstrates how social workers have come to be seen as an important element in the solution to social problems. Beliefs in their expertise and the value of their training have also become widespread. Whenever there is a public inquiry into a scandal or a tragedy, one recurrent recommendation is for more social work training. Richard Titmuss, a leading authority on social policy, commented during a lecture that:

> it is an interesting and often overlooked fact that during the past twenty years whenever the British people have investigated a social problem, there has always followed a call for more trained social workers. (reported in Randall, 1981, p. 222)

But what is the training that differentiates the modern social worker from the charity volunteers of the nineteenth century?

SOCIAL WORK TRAINING

It is not self-evident that social workers need training. Everyone acquires some competence in understanding and helping other people. The first caseworkers employed by the Charities Organisation Society (COS) in the nineteenth century relied on commonsense and practical knowledge to judge whether the paupers applying for alms deserved to be helped. The COS were, however, the first to try and put philanthropy on a scientific footing. In their training, caseworkers were taught to use standards of scientific investigation in their work. They studied applicants' backgrounds to 'diagnose' the causes of their poverty and to decide whether to offer alms or not. They kept detailed records so that the effects of their work could be established. The first major social work textbook *Social Diagnosis* was written by an American caseworker, Mary Richmond, in 1917 explaining the methods developed within the COS. Richmond called it a scientific approach and meant by this that caseworkers should use scientific ways of investigation and recording so that they can develop their own theories about the causes and cures of poverty. She stressed the importance of a thorough exploration of claimant's social circumstances before 'diagnosing' their problems and deciding on 'treatments'. The treatment consisted mainly of arranging financial help and encouraging the clients through a friendly relationship: 'the tonic influence which an understanding spirit always exerts' (Richmond, 1917, p. 200). She did not draw on theories from the social sciences but envisaged that caseworkers would develop theories from their experience. She encouraged caseworkers to keep clear and consistent records of their work so that they could monitor their efforts and then be able to formulate general principles. In 1921, Smith College awarded her an honorary master's degree for 'establishing the scientific basis of a new profession.'

At the turn of the century, social workers turned to science not just for a method of studying clients but as a source of theories. As social workers recognised that solving their clients's problems was no easy task, they looked for better ways of helping them. The natural sciences, with their success in developing theories and effective technologies, offered an inspiring model.

The COS and the Poor Law assumed that the causes of poverty lay within the pauper's control and that avoiding destitution was essentially the individual's responsibility. By the end of the nineteenth century, though, people realised the powerful effect of social and economic factors. Britain experienced an economic depression in the 1880s which created high unemployment, undermining the belief that the unemployed were just workshy. The empirical studies by Charles Booth (1889) in London and Seebohm Rowntree (1902) in York showed how many people were living at or below the subsistence level. Their analysis of the causes of poverty showed that it was not due solely or even mainly to irresponsible behaviour but to a lack of jobs, low wages, illness, and old age – factors the individual could not easily alter.

Recognition of the importance of socio-economic factors influenced social work in two ways, increasing their role and their training. First, there was expanding state intervention in social problems leading to a greater role for social workers, within services for the sick and disabled, in protecting the welfare of children, and within the criminal justice system. Secondly, some pioneering social workers turned to the social sciences for a better understanding of their clients' problems. In 1903 the C.O.S set up a social work course at the new School of Sociology in London (incorporated into the London School of Economics in 1912). Professor Urwick, the director, said in his Introductory Lecture:

There is a new knowledge; in it may be found the
scientific basis for the social education we need; and
it is essential that the worker should learn it. (United
Nations, 1958, p. 110)

At an American social work conference in 1918, Ellwood
argued for using the social sciences:

simple good will and human sympathy are no sufficient guide for the social worker. They may furnish
him with warmth but not with light. (1918, p. 691)

To many caseworkers, however, the practical value of the
social theories seemed very limited. Theories suggested
ways of solving social problems by intervening at the level
of policy but offered little guidance on what to do when
working with individuals and families. Faced with Mrs
Smith who could not feed her children well because her
husband was unemployed, theories might help explain
why there was a recession and a rising unemployment
rate. Appreciating that unemployment was not just due
to the individual's laziness might make caseworkers less
moralistic than their predecessors but this extra understanding did not give them any direct advice on how to
make sure the children got enough to eat. Some social
workers turned their efforts to social reform but for the
majority who continued in direct work, social theories
were little appreciated and had little impact on practice.
Mary Richmond disputed their value:

If I could choose a friend for a family fallen into
misfortune and asking for relief, I would rather
choose for them one who had this practical resource-
fulness than one who had a perfect equipment of
advanced social theories. The former would find the

most natural and effective way out ... the other
would say that the whole social order was wrong and
must pay a ransom for its wrongness by generous
material help for its victims. (Richmond, 1899, p. 137)

Psychology rather than sociology and economics had
the biggest impact on direct practice and produced
another form of social work which was said to be scientific. In what has been called the 'psychiatric deluge'
(Woodroofe, 1962), there was a growing interest in psychiatry and psychology. Psychology in the first half of this
century was dominated by two approaches: the psychoanalytic and the behavioral. Although there have been
advocates of both schools in social work, psychoanalysis
has undoubtedly been the more widely accepted and
used. Social workers, like so many others at the time,
were greatly impressed not only by the deep understanding of human problems these theories offered but also by
their therapeutic promise. Armed with psychoanalytic
training, social workers, it was hoped, would be able to
give their clients a far more effective service. Unlike the
social and economic theories, Freud's focus on the individual blended easily with the social work tradition of
individual and family work.

In the United States of America, where there was a
well-established pattern of training, the psychoanalytic
approach soon became dominant and had a significant
impact on practice; the term 'psychiatric deluge' can be
applied to its effect. In Britain, however, where, in the
1920s and 1930s, few social workers received formal
training, it was considerably less influential (Yellolly,
1980). Nevertheless, it did have a major impact on university-based training courses such as that for psychiatric
social workers at the London School of Economics and
so became the dominant theoretical approach in some
branches of the profession.

Until the 1960s, the dominance of Freudian theories in social work training was only seriously challenged by rival psychoanalytic theories. The curriculum continued to cover social theories but the greatest impact on social work practice theory came from psychoanalysis.

Behaviourism, the main rival to psychoanalysis in psychology, gained more supporters in the 1960s. In Britain, Jehu (1967) produced a textbook for social workers on behaviour modification techniques and introduced them into the training course at Leicester University. In America, many academics adopted the behavioural approach with enthusiasm, impressed by the mounting empirical evidence of its therapeutic effectiveness, which contrasted with the growing evidence against the power of psychoanalytic methods (Reid, 1994, p. 168). Behaviourism has become an element in most training courses now in both Britain and the USA but practitioners have been less enthusiastic about it then academics (Payne, 1991, p. 132). Describing the American response, Reid reports there were concerns about its 'mechanistic' and 'manipulative' character, its making excessive use of external rewards, and its downplaying of the practitioner-client relationship (1994, p. 170).

The supremacy of psychoanalytic theories among trained social workers was ended in the early 1970s when many rival approaches were introduced. Orcutt (1990), discussing the changes in American social work, suggests that the theory base was widened because of the doubts raised by research evidence about the effectiveness of psychoanalytic therapy and psychosocial casework. There were also questions about the suitability of an analytic approach with many of social work's clients to whom help with their practical problems seemed more valuable than talking. These doubts were raised at a time of 'political upheaval and social unrest characterised by opposition to tradition, overturning established patterns, and a general questioning of what had been learned in the past' (Orcutt, 1990, p. 161). Payne offers a similar analysis of British practice with the additional point that social workers rejected psychoanalytic theories because they are strongly deterministic, preferring theories 'which acknowledge the centrality of clients' ability to control their environment' (1991, p. 245).

Numerous alternative approaches were presented, so many indeed that it is hard to list them all. Recent textbooks for social work students (Howe,1987 and Payne, 1991) offer an overview of available methods covering not only the long-standing analytic and behavioural schools but crisis-intervention and task-centred methods, social systems theory, social psychological and communication models, humanist and existential models, and Marxist and feminist approaches. Besides the growth in therapeutic ideas, there has also been an increase in the pool of relevant material from the flourishing social sciences about understanding people and societies. This expansion in the potential knowledge base of social work is reflected in the curricula of training courses.

Nowadays, there is one formal social work qualification – the Diploma in Social Work, which can be obtained by a variety of routes. Many students undertake a two year postgraduate or non-graduate course in a university or college; some do an undergraduate degree; others train while working in a social services post. The Central Council for Education and Training in Social Work (CCETSW) prescribes, in broad terms, the curriculum for training programmes (CCETSW, 1995). Six pages of key areas of knowledge are listed, specifying, *inter alia*, theories of human growth and behaviour; family life cycles; social, family and community structures; theories of welfare; comparative social policies; health, disability and social conditions; causes and effects of crime, mental illness, learning difficulties, AIDS, alcohol and substance abuse; law, statutory duties, powers and legal principles; social work purpose, models, methods, settings and theory; and social work values.

WHICH THEORIES TO USE

The CCETSW guidelines cover vast subject areas. Selection is essential but the social work teacher faces a difficult task. Engineers or technicians who look to the natural sciences for theoretical knowledge find a general consensus about which theories to accept but the social sciences offer a range of conflicting theories, many of which are highly speculative, untested, and controversial. As early as 1965, one American academic was reporting that: 'the embarrassment of riches with which the social work educator today is faced, as new theories about man and society replace or cast shadows of uncertainty on the old' makes deciding on the curriculum 'a Herculean task' (Dana, 1965, p. 6). Since then, the task has only got bigger.

In practice, courses generally teach a range of conflicting and complementary theories but do not come down in favour of any particular one. Sheldon, a social work academic, describes this type of curriculum as the 'supermarket' style of teaching:

> the incoming student takes his 'basket' to each of the various subject displays, selects the goods which take his fancy, and obtains his CQSW at the check-out; his choice is virtually unconstrained. (1978, p. 9)

Recent textbooks make the supermarket analogy appear even more fitting. Howe (1987) and Payne (1991) offer a wide range of theories but leave it to the reader to decide which ones to adopt: the student: 'pays her money and takes her choice' according to Howe (1987, p. 166).

Sheldon goes on to illustrate the choice available on a

typical course with a lighthearted but only slightly carica-
tured account of the student's experience:

> theories are often taught alongside each other, the
> ultimate choice being left to the student. Here, the
> failure of an individual to develop an adequately
> functioning conscience may be discussed on Mondays
> in terms of his early feeding experiences (Klein), on
> Tuesdays, as resulting from a failure to resolve a
> competitive relationship with his father at four
> (Freud); on Wednesdays a disturbance in the discrete
> stages of intellectual development which exert influ-
> ence over the next decade may be indicted (Piaget);
> and on Thursdays the lifelong process of operant
> conditioning is emphasized (Skinner). Friday is for
> fieldwork, of course. (Sheldon, 1978, p. 10)

Commentators on training programmes in the USA
have made similar points. For instance Goldstein, like
Sheldon, illustrates the complex range of ideas confront-
ing students, asking us to:

> consider the plight of the typical recent graduate of a
> social work program whose head is cluttered with
> this diversity of constructs and theories. Where does
> one begin in the attempt merely to assess the client?
> Should the focus be on the client's ego strengths,
> social role, psychosocial patterns, personality traits,
> or status in his or her system? Or, should the focus
> be on the family's interactions, communication pat-
> terns, selected external re-enforcements, or what?
> (Goldstein, 1986, p. 354)

Loewenberg expresses sympathy for the American social
work student:

There are those who wonder whether this unrestrained freedom to choose from a large number of different theories does not put too large a burden on the individual social worker (1984, p. 310).

Little is known about how students choose from the range offered to them but it appears to be essentially a personal decision of what seems convincing to the individual. One possible way to appraise theories is by scientific standards, to ask whether, on the empirical evidence available, they look plausible or have stood up to testing better than their rivals. There are two major difficulties for students wanting to do this. First, they do not appear to receive much teaching on how to evaluate theories scientifically. Cassons made an extensive survey of social work courses in Britain and criticised them for providing little help to students on how to judge theories:

> unless the principles by which knowledge is constructed and tested are made explicit, the student is left with no clear way of comprehending why explanations should conflict and can develop no criteria upon which he can make choices between explanations. A second implication is that the student may attribute a status to knowledge transmitted to him that is not justified by the way it was constructed and tested. (Cassons, 1982, p. 126)

Secondly, theory evaluation is hampered by the lack of empirical evidence for or against them. Social work does not have a strong research tradition and so, particularly in relation to social work practice theories, provides few empirical studies of their use and effectiveness. But this lack of empirical research is not seen as a problem by most students. It seems to be part of the anti-scientific culture that social workers generally do not pay much attention to the empirical studies that are available. There is still far more interest in psycho-analytic theories than behavioural ones despite the wealth of evidence against the power of psycho-analytic therapies and for the effectiveness of behavioural modification techniques.

HOW TO USE THEORIES

There has always been a troublesome relationship between theories and practice in social work. An engineer designing a bridge will use the theories in an explicit systematic way, knowing what theory is being used and checking it is being accurately applied. A doctor prescribing a drug will give a precise amount decided on the basis of extensive clinical trials. Research shows that few social workers use theories in such a formal, explicit way. Most seem to absorb a selection of theoretical ideas into their background knowledge and use it intuitively.

From early on, it was apparent that students did not consciously and explicitly transfer their theoretical training into direct work with clients. Indeed, it was not clear that they used it at all. In 1931, Karpf's study of American social workers found 'little evidence that the caseworker uses any other than the commonsense concepts and judgements' (1931, p. 352):

> The conclusion was fairly clear that despite the testimony of social work literature to the effect that social workers should have special equipment in the form of training in the sciences basic to social work, their case records gave little indication that they have or use any specialised knowledge. (1931, p. 353)

A recent four year study of practice teaching, commissioned by CCETSW, indicates that the difficulties in making clear links between theory and practice continue. It concludes:

> although 'theory' and 'practice' have been posited as the two key elements of social work training, integration of the two remains problematic and elusive. The study found little evidence that they are actively joined together; theory appears to be what goes on in lectures and seminars, while practice is what students do in placements. (Walker *et al*, 1995, p. 2)

Even when theories seem to have some influence, they are not used in a clear, conscious or systematic way. CCETSW, in prescribing training courses, expects qualifying social workers to be able to 'conceptualise, reflect, analyze and critically evaluate both underpinning knowledge and their own practice'. Also 'they should be able to explain in a coherent, comprehensive and convincing manner how their practice is informed by their knowledge base' (1995, p. 5). The findings of research indicate that such a use of knowledge is not often achieved. Most practitioners, studies report, think they are influenced by their theoretical training but are unsure what theories they are using. Several studies have found that when practitioners are asked directly to spell out the theories or therapies they are using, they have great difficulty in responding (Goldberg and Warburton, 1979; Carew, 1979; Corby, 1982, Waterhouse, 1987).

Parsloe and Stevenson, in their study of 31 social service teams, concluded that social workers did not, in general, adopt a clear theoretical approach:

> On the whole, our respondents' descriptions of their work with clients did not suggest that practice was drawn from specific theoretical perspectives. It may

be that they had so internalised theory that they put it into practice without being conscious of it or able to talk about it. One experienced worker commented: 'if you ask me to state a theory here and now, I wouldn't have a clue but my thinking and my approach have been formed by it.' There was some evidence that many of the experienced workers were accustomed to working mainly on the intuitive level – in the sense of responding to the immediate situation without conscious reliance on a theoretical framework. (1978, p. 134)

The suggestion that workers are using theories even though they cannot easily put a label on their way of working is borne out by an interesting study done by Curnock and Hardiker (1979). Besides interviewing practitioners, they studied social enquiry reports prepared by probation officers to see what ideas were influential. Hardiker's (1981) research had a similar aim. She interviewed social workers and examined their assessments of child care referrals, analysing the reports and discussions in terms of their apparent theoretical slant. Both studies found evidence of theories being used in conjecturing the causes of the child care problems or the offending behaviour.

Payne (1991) and Howe (1987) have both argued cogently that the option for social workers is not between using or rejecting theories but between using theories consciously or implicitly. Theoretical assumptions form an intrinsic part of reasoning about clients. Social workers can be either clear or hazy about what assumptions they are making. Howe argues that:

not only is theory in social work unavoidably integral to any practice, but also its relegation to an implicit, unarticulated status leads to a poor, indeed dishonest practice. (Howe, 1987, p. 1)

A recent study of social work students by Secker (1993) provides a more detailed picture of how theories are used and how students' use of them changes during their training. She describes three types of usage – the 'everyday social', the 'fragmented', and the 'fluent'.

The 'everyday social' approach was most commonly found at the start of training where the students drew solely on knowledge derived from their personal everyday lives. At first contact with the client, the emphasis was on establishing a warm, friendly relationship, trying to show a positive, non-critical attitude. Gathering information was a lower priority and the hope was that it would emerge as in the course of an ordinary conversation rather than in an official interview. From this perspective, clients' accounts of their problems were 'regarded as straightforward facts of the case which merited sympathy but no further exploration or interpretation. Indeed to treat them otherwise was perceived to be tantamount to expressing disbelief or disagreement' (1993, p. 36). This friendly, unquestioning approach tended to persist throughout the contact with the client. Further information tended to emerge in a piecemeal way. Students working in this mode found recording their work difficult: 'rather than describing any overall understanding, they offered lengthy, anecdotal descriptions of personalities and events which together had the flavour of stream of consciousness accounts' (1993, p. 41). Because of the non-questioning, non-directive style, these students' success in helping their clients depended on the clients' own ability to identify and address their problems. Unfortunately, the majority of the clients found this difficult, providing support for Ellwood's claim in 1918 that 'simple good will and human sympathy are no sufficient guide for the social worker' (1918, p. 691).

The second type of usage, the 'fragmented' approach, was most apparent in the students' first placements though many never progressed beyond it. Their practice was characterised by conflicts between their everyday knowledge and the theories they were being taught which made them uncertain of how to act with clients. They had difficulty in moving from one conceptual framework to the other. So, in an interview where they wanted both to establish a helping relationship and to obtain the information needed by a specific theory, they had difficulty in combining the two tasks. The first required their ordinary social skills while the latter demanded a more structured approach with the social worker guiding the discussion into the areas he or she wanted to cover. Secker found that students resolved this difficulty by making one task primary and the other secondary.

Some focused on developing the relationship, applying the theory with hindsight not during the course of the interview. They intended to return to collect more information systematically once the relationship was established but, in practice, they found it hard to alter the style of contact they had established with the client. They had particular problems in raising difficult issues such as death or sexuality that are generally considered taboo in ordinary social conversations. Therefore even though they could increase their understanding of the client's problems by drawing on theories outside the interview, they were unable to use this understanding in subsequent contacts but continued to focus on maintaining a helping relationship.

The other way students resolved the problem was to use a theory as a recipe for practice, approaching interviews with a fixed agenda and paying little attention to the nuances of the interactions. They had already formed a theoretical explanation of the client's problems and applied this in an uncritical way: 'instead of exploring or seeking confirmation of the validity of their ideas, the students proceeded straight away to implement the kind of intervention which seemed, rule book fashion, to fit' (1993, p. 66). Most felt uncomfortable with this approach, finding it rigid or robotic and its inflexibility made them feel unresponsive to the clients.

The third usage, the 'fluent' approach, was one that a few students achieved by the end of training where they were able to integrate the different sources of knowledge and use both commonsense wisdom and theories in direct work with clients. Students used theories as a framework 'to simultaneously guide the gathering and interpretation of information' (Secker, 1993, p. 80). Theories were not used in an uncritical way:

> Rather, the students emphasised the importance of assessing the likely validity of their theoretical ideas in the light of the information emerging about a particular situation. If necessary they were then able to shape and adapt their original ideas in order to take into account the particular circumstances of the people with whom they worked. (1993, p. 80)

These students also had a critical attitude to their empathic skills. Empathy was valued but 'students did not take it for granted that their affective responses were an accurate reflection of the feelings and needs of the people with whom they worked ' (1993, p. 81).

'Fluent' students were also able to share their thinking with clients, to tell them what explanations they were developing or what plans they were making: 'they were concerned to ensure that the people with whom they worked were aware of the direction their own thoughts were taking and were able to discuss and contribute to their ideas' (1993, p. 83).

Secker's research is valuable in analysing how social workers practice and showing that there are several significantly different styles in social work. Her three categories of 'everyday social', 'fragmented' and 'fluent' face varying degrees of difficulty in meeting the challenge to say what they are doing and to justify it. The fluent group's ability to explain their ideas and plans to clients suggests that the issue of moving from a private, personal style of working to a more public, accountable one may be at least as much to do with levels of expertise as with philosophical debates about knowledge.

CONCLUSION

The aim of this chapter has been to describe the roles and expertise of social workers. As the profession has moved from the private to the public sector, their roles can be sketched by reference to their statutory responsibilities and powers. But describing their expertise has proved a more complicated task. Everyone develops some skills in understanding their fellow human beings. Since ancient times, people in distress have been helped by receiving practical and emotional support. With the rise of a distinct social work profession, the question arose whether our commonsense wisdom was enough or whether there were more powerful ways of understanding and helping clients. The growth of social work training courses demonstrates growing acceptance that social workers should use theories from the social sciences to enrich their understanding and their methods of practice. Professional training, with a substantial contribution from the social sciences, has developed over the past hundred years so that now over ninety percent of social workers in Britain are qualified.

CCETSW, the professional body responsible for validating training courses, talks of a 'common body of knowledge' but this is misleading. The range of theoretical knowledge offered to students is vast, conflicting, and little tested. It is neither 'common' to all students nor well enough supported by evidence to claim the title of 'knowledge'. Moreover, the teaching of theories does not have a clear, consistent impact on practice. For the most part, students decide for themselves which, if any, theories to accept. Any theory then tends to be absorbed into their background knowledge and used in a piecemeal, unconscious way.

According to CCETSW's guidelines, students are to be encouraged to work in a reflective, goal-oriented way, drawing on theories from the social sciences to understand their clients, using therapeutic methods in a systematic manner, and turning to research for empirical evidence about the accuracy of theories and the effectiveness of therapies. If they did indeed work in this way, social workers would be better prepared to meet the demands that they describe and justify their work. There is however a serious split between this model of practice and the way most practitioners actually function. They develop an individual and private style of working which it is hard for them to express clearly. Research studies have consistently found that, once qualified, social workers appear to make little use of theories in any conscious or systematic way despite the fact that they report that theories are influential. They show little interest in empirical studies, leaving judgements about clients and evaluations of progress mainly to individual practitioners. Within this private style of working, Secker's research has revealed different groups some of whom are far more able to reflect on what they are doing and to communicate it to others.

CHAPTER 3
The Art/Science Debate

Faced with a broken washing machine, most people will have little idea about how to mend it beyond phoning for a repairman who will have the special training and skill to deal with the problem. If we meet a person in distress, on the other hand, most people have some ideas about how to respond, whether or not they have received any formal training. Understanding ourselves and the people around us is a fundamental element of everyday life. People coming into social work as a career, therefore, already have a fund of wisdom and skills in understanding human nature.

As we saw in the preceding chapter, there have been enduring controversies in social work about the value and aims of formal, academic training. The existence of our commonsense understanding has led to debates about what is the appropriate knowledge base for social workers. In everyday life, we use our personal skills of intuition and empathy to understand others, drawing on a wealth of implicit ideas developed from experience. Should social workers use more formal, explicit theories about human behaviour? If so, how can they be integrated into practice? Do they build on our commonsense ideas or do they offer a radically different type of understanding?

There have been similar debates in the social sciences in general. The way we refer to people's mental states, to their beliefs and reasons for acting as they do, has been the central focus of dispute. It seems to some people to conflict with a scientific approach. Astronomers can study the movements of the stars and botanists can dissect plants but other people's thoughts and feelings are not so easily examined. Some (the humanists) have then argued that we cannot use scientific methods in studying human actions. Others (the strict behaviourists) say that we have to reject our commonsense ideas and study people's behaviour, ignoring what is going on in their minds. The majority of social scientists, however, have avoided both these extreme views and taken the line that the basic assumptions we have in everyday life about human actions are perfectly compatible with scientific theories of explanation.

The aims of this chapter are two-fold: first, to link the different social work points of view to the debates in philosophy, and, secondly, to outline where the issues will be developed later in the book. We begin with a more detailed look at our everyday understanding of behaviour as this is the background to the more philosophical issues.

COMMONSENSE PSYCHOLOGY
When a falling branch breaks a window, we wonder what caused it to happen. When a boy breaks a window, we ask why he did it. In everyday life, we think of each other's actions as *intentional*, as done for a purpose. Unlike the movement of a branch, we try to understand human actions in terms of *reasons* not *causes* We want to know people's thoughts, feelings and their intentions which led them to do a particular thing. We see each other as more or less rational people who are responsible

for what we do and whose mental processes, decisions, choices, etc, determine our actions.

The desire to understand ourselves and others pre-dates the social sciences and social work by thousands of years. As we grow up, we are all involved in learning about people and the society in which we live. We all acquire a 'commonsense psychology' which is extensive and, for many everyday purposes, very successful.

One important feature of human behaviour we learn is the distinction between actions and events. Some things happen to us, such as our eyes automatically blinking at bright light, but some types of behaviour seem under our control. We can choose to stand up or sit down; we can plan our future actions. We are not puppets controlled by strings but responsible human beings. There is however no sharp dividing line between actions for which we are responsible and behaviours which are outside our control and this often causes disputes. Social workers face difficult judgements in deciding to what extent a client is respon-sible for his or her actions. Their explanations of behav-iour typically involve elements of both individual responsibility and recognition of external causes (Hardi-ker and Webb, 1979).

Is the mother who is severely depressed fully in control when she hits her baby? Are the crimes of juvenile delinquents partly the result of social forces outside their personal control? Both these examples raise questions about whether the client should be blamed for what happened. This is not surprising because the issue of responsibility is most often raised in moral contexts. In general, we are only held morally responsible for behav-iour we are thought to control so that we could have done something else. It is not sensible to say that someone *should have* done something else unless we also believe that he *could have* taken another course. Inasmuch as it can be shown that someone's ability to exercise free will was restricted then their moral responsibility for their behaviour is also reduced.

When judging whether particular reasons provide an adequate explanation of an action, we assume some kind of rationality principle. Philosophers have found it difficult to formulate this in an uncontentious way but a simple version of it is:

> given any person X, if X wants D and X believes that A is a means to attain D, under the circumstances, then X does A. (Rosenberg, 1988, p. 25)

To use the example of the boy breaking the window, if we are told, perhaps, that he was wanting to get into the house to steal money and believed that this was the easiest way of doing so, then his action becomes intelligible to us. We understand his purpose and how he thought this action would help him achieve it. We might well disapprove of his conduct but it makes sense. If, on the other hand, we were only told that he was trying to catch a bus and therefore broke the window, we would feel puzzled. His action would seem irrational and we would ask more questions. If it transpired that he was wanting to break in to steal money to pay his bus fare then his action becomes understandable.

Social workers often meet clients who say they want to do one thing but actually do something else, like the battered wife who says she wants to leave but, when given the means to do so, in fact keeps returning to the abusive partner. Rather than condemning her as irrational, the social worker usually tries to understand her, to tease out her motives and feelings more so that it becomes apparent that, though she has many sincere reasons for wanting to leave, there are stronger reasons for staying. In looking for such understanding, the social worker is assuming the client is rational, that her actions are intentional and explicable in terms of her beliefs and wishes.

We develop an extensive understanding of people's behaviour. We learn typical patterns of behaviour and social rules which enable us to explain our own and others' actions. But, like social workers, we have difficulty in spelling out our reasoning in detail. To use an example suggested by the American philosopher Hilary Putnam (1978), it might be clear to everyone in a given situation that Jones is jealous of Smith's reputation though we would find it hard to offer a formal account of how we all reached this conclusion. We could point to the evidence we had based our judgement on – the comments Jones had made or the way he had looked at Smith. We would not however want to assert a general law that everyone who says X in situation Y is jealous. We could easily think of many exceptions to such a rule. In a similar setting, Brown might make the same type of comments but we would interpret them differently perhaps because we know that Brown often jokes while Jones is very serious or because we know that Brown's reputation is much higher than Smith's so he has little cause for jealousy. In ordinary life we are not usually asked to provide an in-depth justification of our judgements but if we start to unravel our reasoning, we draw on a vast reservoir of background knowledge about people. Our thinking is intuitive and based on implicit knowledge unlike the explicit formal reasoning found in science.

We have a particular skill in understanding other minds – the power of empathy. Other people's thoughts and feelings are, to some extent, private but we can get close to them by empathising with them. We have the ability to use our own mental experiences to imaginatively enter into another's private mental world, to draw, for instance, on our own experience of sadness to understand how an unhappy friend is feeling. The arts communicate ideas to us in part by relying on our empathic talents. Good literature can make us sense that we are sharing the characters' experience and give us a new insight into how it feels to be in their circumstances. We can be moved to tears or joy by words on a page or acting on a stage.

Empathy can be a mixed blessing in social work. It is not always under our control to be turned on or off at will. It is hard to see someone in severe distress without empathising to some degree and feeling some of their pain. Social workers spend a considerable time with people experiencing the extremes of human suffering and consequently pay an emotional cost themselves for their involvement. When telling parents their children are being taken into care, for example, they cannot help sensing the anguish they are causing, making the task painful for them as well as the family.

Empathy also provides us with a way of judging the adequacy of explanations. If we are told how a person's thinking and feeling led him to act in a particular way, we can imagine ourselves in those circumstances and judge whether the set of information feels coherent and offers a plausible account; whether it feels right .

Commonsense psychology differs from science in several ways. It is based on implicit rather than explicit, formal theories. Conclusions are reached intuitively rather than as a clear deduction from premises. Judgements about the adequacy or truth of explanations are made by the individual who judges whether they seem plausible or feel empathically convincing. The perennial debate in the philosophy of social science has been on whether this commonsense psychology can form the basis for scientific theorising or not. There have been three main philosophical points of view on the question of the relationship between our commonsense psychology and science, all of which have been represented in social work.

The first two, humanism and strict behaviourism, agree that science and commonsense psychology are incompatible. The humanists then argue that scientific methods cannot be used in studying people while strict behaviourists say that scientists must reject our ordinary view of people and study them within a different framework. The third view is that science and commonsense psychology are compatible; scientists can study the mind and intentional behaviour.

THE REJECTION OF SCIENCE

Humanism comes in many forms but three central claims are (a) to understand people's actions, we need to know what is going on in their minds; (b) the mind cannot be studied by the methods of the natural sciences, and (c) empathy provides us with an alternative means of understanding the mind. Humanists claim, moreover, that empathy gives us a distinctively different type of understanding than can be achieved in the natural sciences. Scientists say they understand, for example, the movement of the stars when they offer a causal explanation of them but their theories do not and cannot tell us what it feels like to be a star in motion. Whereas, when we say we understand why a bereaved person cried, we can mean that we know how they were feeling, we can, in a sense, share their experience. Humanists argue that the aim of studying people is to enrich our empathic understanding, not to develop causal theories to explain their conduct.

The humanist view seems a great deal more popular among social workers than any scientific approach to understanding people. Many believe that they can develop expertise in working with clients but this takes the form of improving their intuitive and empathic skills, their practice wisdom, rather than through formal theories. Empathy is widely seen as a major source of understanding, as a way of appreciating how clients view their problems. 'Empathy puts one into the feelings and experiences of the other' (Goldstein, 1986, p. 68). It enables a social worker to 'know the client's problem almost as if he were living it' (England, 1986, p. 23).

Some also claim that empathy is not just a way of understanding but also a means of helping clients. England for example says that 'it is experiencing the empathic helper which is itself the principal therapy' (1986, p. 24). Jordan too sees it as a necessary part of therapy:

> empathy implies that the helper 'feels with' the person in trouble; that by imaginatively entering the other's situation, he engages his own emotions in such a way as to share the other's responses. I am suggesting that this is an essential part of helping. (1979, p. 20)

Few who favour a more scientific approach would deny that empathy is a valuable skill in understanding clients. Nor, if it were possible, would they want social workers to switch off this faculty in their direct work with clients. But the next chapter will argue that empathy has serious limitations as a source of understanding.

THE REJECTION OF THE MIND
The most extreme approach to the scientific study of people has been that of the strict behaviourists. Like humanists, they believe that the mind and mental processes pose difficulties to a scientist but argue that scientists can avoid them by not studying the mind at all but concentrating on what is more readily observed, namely, human behaviour. The leading behavioural psychologist, B.F. Skinner, claims that:

> we do not need to try to discover what personalities, states of mind, feelings, traits of character, plans,

purposes, intentions, or any other perquisites of man really are, in order to get on with a scientific analysis of behaviour. (1974, p. 239)

The view of science implicit in strict behaviourism is probably the most familiar to social workers and widely disliked. Many appear to think it is the only possible scientific approach to social work. Most of the anti-scientific arguments only apply to such a restricted picture of science. 'The self cannot be observed . . . nor can it be measured, so it must be ignored' – this, claims Wilkes (1981, p. 75) is the only possible attitude scientists can take to the human mind. Ragg (1977) and Raynor (1984) both assume that scientific theories cannot explain people's actions in terms of their reasons. Jordan (1979) and Goldstein (1986), too, depict a scientific approach as necessarily limited to the study of behaviour, excluding the mind.

For all these authors, the belief that science cannot study the mind means there is an unbridgeable gap between science and the traditional ways of understanding and helping clients in social work. But they are attacking a straw man, a view of science which few would defend. As Chapter Five will detail, the strict behaviourists' programme of studying only behaviour is not dictated by the demands of scientific method. Scientists do speculate beyond the simply observable and, indeed, do so very profitably. Contemporary theoretical physics, for example, is very largely concerned with the study of unobservable phenomena such as quarks, electrons and super strings. If such strange entities can be the topic of scientific enquiry, our thoughts and feelings, which are far more accessible to us, cannot be excluded on the grounds that they are not directly observed. Excluding the mind is not necessary for scientific study.

Social work critics of science, however, are not unusual

in directing their criticisms at a narrow version of science. Giedymin, reviewing the equivalent debate in the social sciences, reports a similar tendency:

> Contrary to the claims of anti-naturalists (Winch, Wright, for example) none of the naturalists in my survey claims that descriptions in the social sciences (and humanities) are or ought to be purely pheno-menalistic, i.e. in behaviouristic terms, that explanations of human actions are or ought to be mechanistic, without reference to human aims, beliefs, etc. Just the opposite is the case: they all insist that social sciences and humanities are concerned primarily with studying men as ration beings ... they all agree that typical explanations of individual actions in history (and humanities in general) are in terms of aims, intentions, beliefs, available means, existing obstacles, institutional set-ups, etc. (Giedymin, 1975, p. 290)

Social workers' tendency to identify science with strict behaviourism is, to some extent, understandable because this school of psychology has had such a high profile on both sides of the art/science debate in social work. Nowadays, many of those wanting social work to be more scientific also urge social workers to adopt a behavioural approach. But it is its effectiveness, not any claim to being the only possible scientific approach, that wins their support. Its therapeutic developments – behaviour modification techniques – have produced impressive results. Hudson and Macdonald, in their textbook on behavioural social work, offer a moral, not a methodological, argument for using behavioural techniques:

> Being a 'social worker' is different from being a 'friend', and it is important to locate the additional

ethical constraints imposed by the social work role. And in our view the central such view is 'effectiveness'. (1986, p. 9)

From the available evidence, Hudson and Macdonald conclude that behaviourism is the most effective. Brewer and Lait, while making a strong case for behavioural social work, make it clear that their essential plea is that social workers should be concerned to check the effectiveness of their services: 'we would welcome any other approach which can be shown to be effective' (1980, p. 101).

THE MIND AND SCIENCE

The third philosophical view on the relationship between commonsense psychology and science argues that there is no incompatibility: the workings of the mind can be studied scientifically. This has been the most dominant view in the social sciences.

Most social scientists have long accepted the need to study people's thinking in order to explain their behaviour. Social sciences study people' actions, social organisations, and belief systems; a central feature of all of these is that what they are depends, in part, on the beliefs and intentions of the people involved. To say that a man is 'voting for Smith' is not just to describe his physical movements of putting a cross in the relevant place on the ballot paper but assumes that he has the appropriate knowledge about the voting system and the intention of showing his support for Smith. A child, playing around, might put a cross next to the name of Smith but he would not be voting. A description of behaviour alone is insufficient to tell us what action is being performed. Mental phenomena, therefore, seem to most social scientists to play an essential role in theories. But views of how the mind can be studied empirically have changed dramatically in recent decades as the positivist philosophy of science has been rejected.

To add to social workers' confusion about science, positivism in the social sciences is also called behaviourism but it is significantly different from the strict behaviourism of Watson and Skinner. Positivists thought that there was a sharp difference between behaviour and mental states. Behaviour, they believed, could be directly observed and described in non-theoretical language. It was therefore classed as empirical. Mental states and processes, however, were considered conjectural and so classed as theoretical. Since science requires theories to be tested by empirical evidence, positivists argued that only reports of behaviour could provide satisfactory evidence to test theories scientifically. They believed that the mind could figure in theories about human actions but reports about the mind could not provide evidence for testing such theories. So social scientists could theorise, for instance, about how early attachment to one's mother affected functioning as an adult but had to test these ideas by collecting evidence of people' behaviour. This is a major shift from the strict behaviourist position which banned any mention of the mind but it is also a long way from commonsense psychology in insisting on checking all hypotheses about the mind against behavioural evidence.

The positivist view of science has been very influential in social work, particularly in the way research has been conducted. Social workers are familiar with researchers' demands for 'facts' and 'hard evidence' – by which was generally meant behavioural evidence. Tripodi, in his textbook on research methodology for social workers, asserts that observations of behaviour are the only acceptable form of empirical evidence: 'observations cannot be used to describe directly the moods and attitudes of clients' (1983, p. 82). Social work researchers like Tripodi have argued that their methodology can be applied to non-behavioural approaches to social work practice. The intuitive and empathic skills that social workers value so highly are allowed a place as a source of theories but they are only speculative and need to be tested by empirical (behavioural) evidence.

Although positivist methodology imposed no ban on psychological concepts, the demand for behavioural evidence placed a serious constraint on researchers. Many have complained that this requirement had a major influence on the choice of topics for research. Finding an issue that could be easily measured in behavioural terms took priority over deciding which issues really mattered to social workers. Weik, an American researcher, claims that positivist research has been 'either solving the wrong problem or solving a problem not worth solving' (1987). Ruckdeschel and Farris complain that positivist researchers: 'have made a ritual of measurement and therefore cannot answer the questions that are relevant for effective practice' (1982, p. 275). Another researcher, Heineman, makes a similar charge:

> In a misguided attempt to be scientific, social work has adopted an outmoded, overly restrictive paradigm of research. Methodological rather than substantive requirements determine the subject matter to be studied. As a result, important questions and valuable data go unresearched. (1981, p. 371)

The results of positivist research have been of limited value to social workers. The major studies of effectiveness discussed in Chapter One, for instance, had undoubted value in alerting social workers to their failure to achieve expected goals. But their concentration on measuring outcomes, with little attention to the far more complex problem of describing the social work service being evaluated, reduces their value as a source of ideas on how to change.

Current post-positivist philosophies of science, while differing on details, agree on certain issues. They portray science as a more creative, conjectural and fallible process than positivism did. One change, which is central to the social work debate, is that the positivist's sharp distinction between theory and observation is shown to be wrong and is replaced with a continuum of more or less theoretical statements. Science is not based on a bedrock of infallible reports of direct observation; statements that are considered empirical presuppose some theoretical assumptions and could, logically, be false. This has major implications for research methodology since it dislodges behavioural evidence from its alleged inherent superiority to psychological reports.

These developments in philosophy have had substantial practical impact on social work research. The most vociferous critics of positivist research are not humanists but researchers. All of the critics just quoted are not hostile to science but to the discredited positivist account of it. There have been numerous articles on this subject in the American literature in the past ten years but it is noticeable that any disagreements concern the implications of rejecting positivism. No-one is defending it. Most seem to agree that early research was unduly narrow and of limited practical value. Many, however, claim that they have absorbed the new ideas from philosophy and the criticisms no longer apply to recent research. Geismar, for instance, describes the criticisms as 'a game of putting up and shooting down straw men' (1982). Sheldon also thinks the complaints are off the mark in claiming that current research ignores the 'softer', psychological evidence:

Most of the American and all of the British research combine these binary type 'yes/no', greater/lesser

'hard' indicators (i.e. outcome measures) with qualitative measures drawn from interviews with clients
and their families. That they do not is a defensive
myth. (1986, p. 230)

As will be discussed in Chapter Six, the revised empiricist
view of empirical evidence offers a more liberal methodology for social work researchers in which qualitative as
well an quantitative data have a valued place. It also
provides a more feasible standard for social work practitioners to aspire to in collecting evidence in their direct
work with clients.

RELATIVISM

Recent philosophy of science has shown more interest in
the social context in which scientists work than previously.
The general public often view scientists as working in a
pure, value-free environment, intent on a disinterested
search for truth, unswayed by any worldly considerations.
But science is a major social activity and affected by the
world around it. The question of which research is funded,
for instance, is a highly political one. In some political
climates, it may be relatively easy to find money to test a
theory that juvenile delinquency is related to single-
parent families while those wanting to test a theory
relating crime to unemployment may search in vain for
funding.

Empiricists would admit the influence of social and
psychological factors in many aspects of science but claim
that empirical testing provides one important area in
which it is value-free. Social factors may make a theory
look plausible, and make scientists anxious to test it but
the empirical evidence provides an independent test.
Politicians may provide the money but they will not make
the tests produce the results they want. Water will boil at
a hundred degrees centigrade whether they like it or not.

This claim is, however, disputed by some who argue that the whole scientific enterprise is undermined by the defects of the positivist account of science. Relativists maintain that science does not produce more reliable knowledge than any other form of reasoning. Scientific methods have no epistemological superiority; they are highly valued in some cultures, including ours, but there is no rational justification for this perceived pre-eminence.

This relativist view of science has far-reaching implications in social work. It has been used to offer a new defence of social workers' hostility to science and preference for a personal, private style of working. Decisions about truth or falsity, probability or improbability, are no longer seen to be decided by reference to empirical evidence but by social and personal factors. Relativists describe science as neither better nor worse than the humanist tradition but just less popular. Social workers, they argue, should stop worrying that their preferred way of working is in some way inferior to scientific reasoning; they should no longer 'feel guilty about the subjective judgements for which they can offer no theoretical justification' (Paley, 1987, p. 170).

Howe also illustrates the repercussions of adopting relativism in social work. He has written an introductory textbook on social work theories for students which, taking a relativist line, relegates scientific methods to being one among many equally valid ones, likely to be attractive to certain personality types. In presenting theories, he does not consider any questions about their truth or probability. The decisions about which theories to use are left to the individual student who 'pays her money and takes her choice' (1987, p. 166). Her decision, though, Howe thinks, will be influenced by her social context: 'Theories', he claims, 'emerge as products of their time and place' (1987, p. 167).

The philosopher most often cited by social workers to

support a relativist position is Thomas Kuhn whose first
book on scientific methods, 'The Structure of Scientific
Revolutions', made a big impact in the social sciences.
This early work has been severely criticised and Kuhn
himself has revised his views substantially, in particular,
arguing against the relativist interpretation of his philosophy. This is examined in detail in Chapter Eight.

CONCLUSION

The role of scientific methods in social work has always
been controversial. To some, science is an ally, a method
by which social workers can develop the most effective
and reliable ways of helping clients. It also produces
public, testable theories which can be used to explain and
justify what social workers are doing. Others, however,
regard science with hostility, fearing that it is incompatible with their views on how to understand and help a
fellow human being.

If the knowledge base of social work is, as the humanists claim, essentially represented in the individual's
empathic and intuitive skills, then we can understand why
so many work in a private and personal way. It is hard for
them to meet the current demands from the public and
from management to be explicit about what they are
doing and to provide evidence to justify their expertise.
But are these personal skills incompatible with attempts
to develop explicit formal theories about how they are
trying to help clients? Social workers' rejection of science
depends on what they think is entailed in being scientific.

Social workers need to learn to formulate their wisdom
in order to meet demands for accountability and to
evaluate their practice more stringently. The way that
most social workers rely on their empathic and intuitive
skills and a personal body of implicit background knowledge is typical of the way we all reason in everyday life.
The task they face in explaining and justifying what they

are doing raises the same issues as in the long-standing debate between humanists and scientists about how to study people.

There is an unbridgeable gap between social workers' concern with understanding the client's mental experience and the strict behaviourists' plan of studying people without any reference to what was going on in their mind. The gap is narrower between social workers' position and that of general behaviourism which allows mental states and processes to feature in theories. The positivist requirement that all such theories must be tested against behavioural evidence has imposed a restriction on researchers that is generally agreed to have, in practice, had a damaging impact on the ability of researchers to tackle the issues of major importance to social workers. The more recent empirical accounts of science offer a more liberal methodology which can be used to develop, not destroy, the currently dominant approach to social work practice.

The conflicting views in the art/science debate are apparent in the development of the social work profession. Those who have argued for a scientific approach have succeeded inasmuch as it has become widely accepted that the social sciences have a valuable contribution to make in social work. These theories however are not then used in a scientific way. The influence of the anti-science view is demonstrated in the way that most practitioners continue to work within the framework and with the reasoning methods of commonsense psychology, absorbing theories into that source of wisdom and continuing to rely mainly on their personal skills of empathy and intuition in their practice.

CHAPTER 4

The Role of Empathy

Empathy gives us a vivid understanding of other people. When a client tells us of his sadness or anxiety, we know how this feels. When children are taken from their familiar home setting to a foster home, we can imagine the emotional impact this has on them. Indeed, being aware of clients' pain is a major motive for wanting to help them. The skill of empathy distinguishes the caring professions from those who work with machines. A repairman who understands washing machines does not know how it feels to be one nor does he need to worry about the emotional impact of his repair work. Our relationships with other people are both enriched and complicated by the power of empathy. It is highly valued by social workers as a source of understanding but, this chapter argues, it has limited scope, power and reliability and needs to be integrated into a more rigorous approach to practice.

A famous quote from the Cleveland Report (HMSO, 1988) is that 'the child is a person not an object of concern'. This report examined an unusual rise in the number of children diagnosed as being sexually abused and removed from their parents in Cleveland. It complained that professionals had paid too little attention to the feelings of the children themselves and made little effort to appreciate what damaging effect the actions of professionals might have on them. It asserted that 'those who work in this field [of child sexual abuse] must have an empathy with children' (1988, p. 252).

The Orkney Report (HMSO, 1992), on another large-scale removal of children thought to be sexually abused, had similar criticisms. In their concern to protect the children, the professionals gave too little consideration to whether they themselves might be inflicting pain. Yet it does not need specialist training or experience to imagine the distress felt by a child in the Orkneys removed without warning from his home and parents, not allowed to speak to his siblings who were also taken away, and not allowed to take his favourite teddy bear or comfort blanket. There were good forensic reasons for this style of removal and perhaps, even after consideration of its effect on the children, it might still have been thought to be the best strategy. However there is no evidence that social workers in Orkney did consider the children's feelings or whether there was a less painful way of protecting them from harm. Empathy therefore can be a useful check on other aspects of practice. Social workers closely involved in carrying out a plan can get so involved with practical details that they overlook the impact they are having on the people they are trying to help.

Empathy is also valuable during interviews as an immediate way of trying to understand the dynamics of the interaction between the client and social worker, of sensing how the client is reacting to comments and how he or she experiences the problems they have. It can trigger new insights into the client's possible feelings and thoughts.

It is hard to stifle one's empathic skill and so, as well as having value as a source of understanding, empathy can also be a source of pain for social workers. Social workers cannot in general tinker with other people's lives as if they were machines. They are aware of the effect they are having and, in some circumstances, the distress they are causing. Carrying out their duties can hurt. The Cleveland Report (1988) acknowledged this repercussion of empathising and recommended that it needed to be taken into consideration in helping staff cope with the stress of dealing with child sexual abuse. Nor should it be seen as a failure, the report suggested, if because of it someone said that he or she was not suited to that area of work.

But empathy in social work is not just used to trigger ideas about the subjective experience of clients. The dominant style of practice described in Chapter Two also uses it as a form of testing. In appraising their practice or an explanation of a client's actions, social workers often judge it empathically, deciding whether it 'feels right', or plausible, to them. Elks and Kirkhart's (1993) small qualitative study of how social workers evaluate their practice provides interesting detail of this use of empathy. The social workers they talked to admitted it was difficult to demonstrate their effectiveness to clients and others. 'Evaluation' meant 'scientific evaluation' to them: 'it was clear that evaluation was equated by the practitioner with science, measurement, and research methodology' (1993, p. 556). 'Nevertheless, the practitioners appeared confident about their effectiveness and saw no need to change' (1993, p. 556). Their confidence arose from their self-appraisal which was based on emotion and intuition. They described their way of judging progress in terms such as: 'I've got to tell you it comes down to a great feeling' and 'I evaluate what I do emotionally' (1993, p. 557). They seemed aware of two standards of evaluation: a scientific one according to which they could not prove their worth, and an intuitive one which gave them the psychological feeling of confidence in their practice.

While not denying that empathy plays a useful role in

social work, I would argue that it has serious limitations. Its fallibility is an obvious cause for concern. Another constraint is that it is not a sufficient form of understanding; it does not satisfy all the legitimate questions we may raise about why people act as they do. But, first, let us consider objections to the claim that it is a powerful and sufficient form of therapy.

THE POWER OF EMPATHY

Just as some humanists have argued that the goal of the social sciences is not to find causal explanations but to understand people empathically, so some social workers have claimed that empathic understanding is the way to help clients. The experience of being empathically understood by a fellow human being is said to provide the supportive setting in which clients in trouble can reflect on their difficulties and find a solution.

The most influential account of this view within social work has probably been the 'client-centred therapy' of Carl Rogers (1957 and 1961), a psychotherapist. England (1986), Goldstein (1986), Jordan (1979) and Wilkes (1981) have presented similar views, all sharing a belief that people have a great capacity for solving their own problems. Therapists, they say, can help by providing the right setting in which our natural drive towards growth and development can be fully realised; therapists do not need any special knowledge or scientific expertise to bring about change.

Rogers for instance believes that we are all striving for 'self-actualisation' and, given the right kind of helping relationship, we can explore our thoughts and feelings and work out new ways of resolving any problems we face:

> the individual has within himself the capacity and the tendency, latent if not evident, to move forward

toward maturity. In a suitable psychological climate this tendency is released ... It is evident in the capacity of the individual to understand those aspects of himself which are causing him pain and dissatisfaction .... It shows itself in the tendency to reorganize his personality and his relationship to life in ways which are regarded as more mature. (Rogers, 1961, p. 35)

After studying the types of relationship that promote improvement, Rogers concluded that there were four important factors: the therapist should show empathy, unconditional positive regard, and genuineness towards the client and the client should recognise that the therapist was displaying these qualities. The therapist variables which have become known as the 'core conditions' of counselling were amplified as follows:

'Empathy' refers to the ability of the therapist to sense accurately the client's feelings and thoughts and to appreciate their significance. 'To sense the client's private world as if it were your own, but without ever losing the "as if" quality – this is empathy' (Rogers, 1957, p. 98).

In showing 'unconditional positive regard', the therapist communicates a positive, non-judgemental acceptance of the client's experience. He or she is valued as a person regardless of any evaluation of their conduct. 'To the extent that the therapist finds himself experiencing a warm acceptance of each aspect of the client's experience as being a part of that client, he is experiencing unconditional positive regard' (Rogers, 1957, p. 98).

Therapists who are 'genuine' express only the thoughts and feelings that they really have; they do not adopt a 'professional' manner that disguises their real reaction to the client. 'The therapist should be, within the confines of this relationship, a congruent, genuine, integrated person ... within the relationship he is freely and deeply himself, with his actual experience accurately represented by his awareness of himself' (Rogers, 1957, p. 97).

While Rogers lists three core conditions of counselling, most other writers single out empathy in particular as the main therapeutic element. Being empathically understood is 'the principal therapy' (England, 1986, p. 24) and 'an essential part of helping' (Jordan, 1979, p. 20).

Carl Rogers and the other advocates of empathy make optimistic claims about its therapeutic power. Rogers claims that a relationship which contains his three core conditions provides: 'the necessary and sufficient conditions of therapeutic personality change. (1957, p. 95). But what evidence is there to support their contention?

Their main appeal is to our own experience. 'We can recognise this in our own experiences of seeking help' says Bill Jordan (1979, p. 21). 'We know from our own experience that this [being empathically understood] is a necessary attribute of the helping person' claims Hugh England (1986, p. 24). And indeed, I expect that most people can think of occasions when such empathic understanding did seem to make it easier to cope with a problem or think of a way of tackling it.

Some value is attached to the quality of the relationship in every therapeutic approach. Both behaviourists and psychoanalysts for instance accept that the nature of the therapist/client relationship influences the effectiveness of their therapies. Freud (1912) held that, for psychoanalysis to work effectively, the therapist needed to form a 'working alliance' with patients. This alliance was based, he thought, on patients recognising that the therapist was understanding and well disposed towards them. If patients experienced warm and positive feelings from the therapist, Freud suggested, they were more likely to respond well whatever therapy was being used. Similar views are found in behavioural textbooks where a positive relationship is seen as important in helping communication and motivating the patient in therapy (e.g. Hawton *et al*, 1989, p. 5).

The claim that empathy is *sufficient* as therapy is far more controversial however and has been the subject of a substantial body of research. Carl Rogers believes that empirical research is essential for developing effective therapeutic services and has therefore encouraged empirical testing of his theory. Most of the research has not been on client centred therapy itself but on the implication of his theory that, whatever method is being used, therapists who score highly on the core conditions would be successful while those with low scores should have low success rates. Rating scales for the core conditions developed by Truax and Carkhuff (1967) have been widely used in the research. Studies have not been on social work clients but on people receiving psychotherapy.

The first reports on the research were very positive. In a review of fourteen studies, Truax and Mitchell (1971) concluded that Rogers' hypothesis had been strongly corroborated. Moreover therapists who scored badly on the core conditions seemed to harm their patients, having a higher degree of deterioration. These positive conclusions are often cited by social workers as evidence for the view they are advocating (e.g. Goldstein, 1973, p. 67, England, 1986, p. 24, and Howe, 1987, p. 5). But they do not take account of the fact that these apparent confirmations were quickly disputed and serious doubt was cast on their reliability.

On closer analysis, it was argued, the studies did not provide the strong support claimed by Truax and Mitchell. As Garfield and Bergin tactfully expressed it, they: 'de-emphasized findings that did not coincide with those predicted by Rogers' hypothesis' (1978, p. 245). For example, Rogers claims that all three conditions are necessary but the studies did not bear this out. Indeed in some cases, low levels of one condition were associated with improved outcome. A study of forty people in hospital with schizophrenia found that those whose therapist showed low levels of genuineness improved more than those who exhibited high levels (Truax, Carkhuff, and Kodman, 1965).

In 1973, Mitchell published a re-analysis of the fourteen studies concluding that the evidence in favour of Rogers' hypothesis was much weaker than he had first judged. His original claim that it was strongly supported is unwarranted in the light of the following statistics. In measuring the correlation between each core condition and patient outcome, he reported that of 109 correlations between empathy and outcome, only 24 were significantly positive, of 108 correlations between warmth and success, 34 were significantly positive, and, in relation to genuineness, 26 out of 88 correlations were found to be positive. Moreover, in 6 cases, genuineness was found to be negatively correlated with success.

Later research continued to produce conflicting results. Some studies provided some support for Rogers' theory; others found a correlation between only one core condition and therapeutic success; some found no correlation. In a further review in 1977, Mitchell reached an even more subdued conclusion:

> the recent evidence, although equivocal, does seem to suggest that empathy, warmth, and genuineness are related in some way to client change but that their potency and generalizability are not as great as once thought. (1977, p. 481)

Research interest in Rogers' theory has waned as the evidence seems to be against it. Some conclusions though are generally agreed to have been demonstrated by the evidence. The strong claim that a relationship containing the core conditions is *sufficient* for therapeutic success is refuted by the results. Even the claim that they are *necessary* is not corroborated but it does seem plausible that their presence may increase the chances of improve-ment, whatever the theoretical orientation of the therapist.

In view of this evidence, one may conclude that social workers' empathic skill may be valuable in increasing their effectiveness but, on its own, it offers a very limited way of helping people.

THE SCOPE OF EMPATHY

Let us now consider the scope of empathy as a source of understanding. First, to what extent can social workers empathise with their clients? Generally, empathy is not thought to be restricted to times when we believe we have had an identical experience. If this were so, it would have very limited scope. Hugh England (1986) makes a typical claim when he suggests that we can empathise when we are able to make a 'link' between the other person's experience and our own:

> He [the social worker] only knows the character of his client's meanings because he himself knows, in general, what it is to experience such mental or emotional states and can sensitively extrapolate from them . . . . He understands confusion not because he has experienced *this* confusion but because he has been confused; he understands loss, depression or love because of his own experience of loss, depression or love. (1986, p. 28)

But how much similarity is needed before we can make a link? The people social workers try to help often have extreme or unusual experiences. Some clients report sensations that find no echo in the life of the typical social worker – the psychotic experiences of someone with schizophrenia for example. Other clients may describe experiences that only partially resonate with our own. Suppose we wish to understand a mother who has assaulted her child. We may be able to empathise with the anger and frustration she felt at the time. Social workers who also have young children may find this particularly easy. But can they then empathise with the experience of venting that rage on a child by physically attacking him? Their own experience would normally be restricted to feeling that fury but controlling it.

Indeed this example illustrates a pervasive feature of social work: people often become clients because they are out of the ordinary; they are the parents who have lost control or the teenagers who have given in to the temptations of crime. We may be able to empathise to some extent but the very nature of their difficulties often means that their experiences are outside the common.

Those who argue that empathy is the central skill in social work believe that it can supply all necessary understanding of other people and see little value in theories from the social sciences. For them, clients' perception of their experience becomes the only accurate version so that theories that offer an explanation that goes beyond this self-understanding are deemed unnecessary or even positively harmful if it affects the quality of the relationship. The behaviourist, for instance, may re-classify a client's feeling of fear as a conditioned response and link it to stimuli in a way the client has not thought of for himself. Psycho-analysts also re-interpret a client's own version of private experiences in the context of unconscious processes outside the client's direct awareness. But to Rogers, Goldstein and others, the client's own understanding is superior to all these formal theories:

No approach which relies upon knowledge, upon training, upon the acceptance of something that is *taught*, is of any use .... If I can provide a certain type of relationship, the other person will discover within himself the capacity to use that relationship for growth, and change and personal development will occur. (Rogers, 1961, p. 32)

Given the right therapeutic relationship, Goldstein claims, clients themselves 'are capable of redefining and resolving the obstacles that block the path toward a more rewarding and confirming existence' (1986, p. 5).

Ragg urges social workers to look to clients not the social sciences for understanding:

At the heart of treating people as people is the necessity of recognising them as the *only source of knowledge* about what they are trying to do. (1977, p. 60, emphasis added)

To this group of writers, science has little place in social work. Social workers may claim expertise inasmuch as their ordinary empathic skills are particularly well developed. They can also achieve specialist understanding, not shared by the general population, because they work with people in unusual or extreme circumstances. They may, for example, have particular awareness of the experience of coping in extreme poverty, or of how parents feel when they learn that their child is severely handicapped. They cannot and should not, however, aim at expertise that builds on the formal theories of the social sciences.

But why should we exclude any other source of understanding? Why should we accept that empathically understanding a client should answer all our questions about why they feel and act as they do? The philosopher Ernest Nagel argues that empathic understanding is not enough (1961, p. 484). It does not satisfy our curiosity about someone's behaviour and, in fact, Nagel points out, does little to answer our questions. In my example of the mother who injured her child, empathy may help to make her actions seem familiar and intelligible to us because, from our own experience, we have noticed that anger and frustration often go with at least a desire to hit out. But knowing that anger and abuse often occur together does not in itself offer a satisfactory explanation of the abuse. As social workers, we would want to know *why* the mother had got into that state, why she did not control her anger as most parents do, and whether she is likely to abuse her child again. In social work, understanding is not an end in itself but a means to an end – of helping the client. Social workers have to *act*, to make assessments and decisions about the child's welfare and this involves reasoning beyond an understanding of the client's experience.

Even when we empathically understand someone, we may still have many legitimate questions about their actions that are unanswered. Typically, answers to these questions can be found by turning to the social sciences. Sociological and psychological theories can add to our understanding by offering an explanation of why the person is experiencing life as he or she is. A theory of loss, for example, places a grieving person's subjective experience at one time into a sequence, explaining how people react to bereavement and work through their grief. The scope of empathy is limited by our ability to make links between our own experience and that of clients. It is also limited to understanding clients' conscious experience and may not provide an answer to legitimate questions about why they feel as they do and how we can help them change. The social sciences provide theories that augment our empathic understanding. The research discussed in Chapter Two indicates that most social workers do draw on social science theories in practice although their use of them is piecemeal and often unconscious.

THE RELIABILITY OF EMPATHY

To philosophers, the main fault with empathy has always been its unreliability. Empathy requires us to make a link between our own experience and that of the other person's. How can we tell whether we are making accurate links? Is a white, middle class, female, social worker able to judge reliably the similarities between her experiences and those of a young, black, working class man? Even if some element is correctly seen as similar, how far can we assume that their reaction to that shared experience will be the same? If two people disagree in their empathic understanding of a third person, how are we to settle the dispute? Difficulty in finding satisfactory answers to these questions has led most philosophers to take the view that empathy is valuable as a source of ideas but, because of its unreliability, these ideas need to be checked independently.

There has always been some feeling of unease among social workers about the accuracy of their empathic skills. The class difference between many social workers and their clients has been seen as a possible source of misunderstanding. More recently, differences in ethnic background have caused social workers to question the reliability of their understanding, fearing that racist prejudices held by white social workers may be distorting work with black clients. Few social workers consciously hold racist views but, it is argued, their ability to empathise can be distorted by false beliefs about other cultures. When empathising, they draw on their background knowledge acquired through their life but most have been brought up in Britain, a pre-dominantly white society with an imperial history and a strong tradition of feeling superior to black people. Their background knowledge therefore may well contain many assumptions that reflect these racist prejudices and so distort their attempts to understand black clients.

Child abuse inquiries also provide examples of faulty empathising. Social workers who had developed a close relationship with abusing families over a long period reported feeling that they had a good understanding and were confident that the parents were not abusing their children nor were they likely to do so. The subsequent death of the child, however, shows that they were seriously wrong. Social workers seemed to have particular difficulty in assessing risk accurately when the parents were charming or appealing in some way. The inquiry into Lucy Gates' death found that the social worker and other professionals 'believed in a fundamental assumption that people with likeable qualities, without insight and ability, are incapable of harming their children' (London Borough of Bexley and Greenwich and Bexley Area Health Authority, 1982, Part Two, p. 157). Stephanie Fox's parents impressed professionals with their intelligence and charm. The inquiry concluded this distorted their judgement when appraising the explanations the parents offered for Stephanie's numerous injuries.

In these cases, close emotional involvement with the parents appeared to be a source of bias rather than a good source of understanding. The inquiries on the whole did not blame the social workers alone for this distortion in their reasoning but saw it as an inevitable and predictable aspect of practice. Most criticism was directed at senior social workers for not providing the necessary help in supervision to enable the workers in direct contact to distance themselves from the family and to test their judgements about them against other sources of evidence.

The attitude to empathic understanding shown in child abuse inquiry reports is the same as most philosophers'.

Empathy is a valuable source of ideas about a person but it is unreliable. The understanding acquired through empathising therefore needs to be treated as tentative and subjected to further testing.

CONCLUSION

Empathising with others is, for most people, a natural part of human relationships. It is a valuable component of social work practice, providing an immediate and rich type of understanding. In the swift interchange of an interview, it is indispensable and unavoidable as a way of sensing what clients are feeling and how they are reacting to the social workers' comments. It also provides a check on other forms of practice, ensuring that the client's subjective experience is not forgotten in considering the options and deciding on the best way to help the client.

Humanists have argued that empathic understanding is the only goal of studying people' actions and, in social work, some have argued that it is the essential skill, removing any need for a knowledge base derived from the social sciences. Its role is limited however. Some contend that its therapeutic power is such that empathy alone is sufficient to provide the setting in which people can resolve their problems. Research evidence tells against this strong claim though it suggests that feeling that the therapist empathically understands you may increase the effectiveness of other methods of helping.

As a source of understanding, empathy is limited to informing us of what is going on in the conscious mind of the other person. This degree of understanding leaves many vital questions unanswered. Knowing how clients feel is not sufficient to deal with all the queries a social worker may have about why they feel as they do and what can be done to help them. The social sciences offer alternatives frameworks into which clients' accounts can be fitted and explained.

The main limitation of empathy, though, is its fallibility. We can claim to know how someone else is feeling because we ourselves have experienced that emotion or sensation. To link their experience to our own, we have to conjecture about what they are feeling from the cues provided, by their words, their actions, and their circumstances. People may differ radically in what they sense another person is feeling but it is hard to resolve conflicts of empathic understanding. A conjecture can be checked to some extent with the client, asking whether your understanding is accurate. This itself is a fallible type of corroboration, especially in the branches of social work, such as child protection, where the client may have strong motives to conceal their true state from their social worker.

Empathy offers a unique source of ideas to help us understand other people and it is a resource not available to physicists or chemists studying non-human phenomena. Only strict behaviourists would deny its value to the social scientist but it offers such a limited and fallible type of understanding that it needs to be augmented and independently tested.

CHAPTER 5

Creative Thinking and Theories

To become more scientific, the first step is for social workers to make their knowledge base explicit. Science obviously provides one model of an explicit knowledge base but many social workers think that the understanding they acquire through their close involvement with clients is significantly different from the theories scientists formulate as a result of their objective study of data. Their view of science however is misleading in several important respects and, far from being opposites, the ideas implicit in practice wisdom can be seen as similar to scientists' initial speculations and efforts to develop an explicit, testable theory. Practice wisdom can therefore be seen as a first stage in theory development. The history of science, however, also illustrates how theorising is a difficult enterprise requiring imagination and intelligence. While science offers a feasible model for social workers for developing a public knowledge base, it provides no simple, mechanical way of creating theories.

The faulty image of science in social work is re-enforced by two major factors. First, the popular layperson's image of scientists is of cool, unemotional people studying 'the facts' in a detached and objective manner. In contrast, social workers are caring helpers, involved in a close relationship with clients, using their hearts as well as their heads as they try to understand their problems. Secondly, this image, while untrue of most branches of science, does resemble strict behaviourism which is the scientific approach most prominent in social work. Since it advocates excluding study of the human mind from psychology, it is not surprising that so many social workers think science is a radically different discipline from their approach to understanding people.

'Simple inductivism' is the philosophy implicit in the common perception of science. It is often called 'Baconian science' after the seventeenth century philosopher Francis Bacon (though it has been argued that it is an inaccurate reading of his work (Urbach, 1987)). The standard interpretation of his writing is that he thought that scientists began by amassing a set of facts, either by casual observation or deliberate experiment. They studied these facts, looking for regularities and correlations, and then employed a set of inductive rules so simple that practically anybody could use them to develop true theories. There is no need for creative leaps of the imagination or flashes of inspiration. Scientific method, according to this view, is both mechanical and infallible.

This account of science is appealing. In view of the heat and controversy so many social issues arouse, it would be attractive if we could cast aside all prejudices and preconceptions and approach the subject in a neutral way; if we could observe all the evidence and build a theory explaining, for example, criminal behaviour, unbiased by our political views or our feelings about crime and criminals. Unfortunately, science is not such a mechanical process and scientists cannot be so neutral. The first section in this chapter explains the faults of Baconian philosophy and details current philosophical views on scientific theorising. I then discuss the rationale behind strict behaviourists' exclusion of the mind from psychology and show how their resulting methodology differs markedly from most branches of science. Another common objection to trying to develop scientific theories in social work is that the scientific search for causal explanations of human actions is somehow inconsistent with the general belief that we have free will. I argue that the notions of causality and freedom are compatible. The final section shows that the way social workers reason about their clients drawing on their practice wisdom is, in all important respects, similar to the way scientists theorise. There is no logical barrier to making their wisdom explicit in the form of tentative theories that can be subsequently tested and revised.

THE MYTH OF THE NEUTRAL OBSERVER

One crucial fault in the common picture of scientists is the idea that it is possible to study the world from a neutral standpoint. In the Baconian account of science, it is thought that scientists approach their subject without any pre-existing ideas, producing theories based on their observations alone, uninfluenced by preconceptions and biasses. There is a false belief that, as the philosopher O'Hear puts it, scientists 'approach nature with an innocent and uncorrupted eye' (1989, p. 14).

Echoes of this belief can be found in social work writing. Theorists often advise social workers to make a sharp distinction between neutral fact-gathering and theoretical interpretation of the facts. Mary Richmond in 'Social Diagnosis', the first social work textbook, tells practitioners that: 'in social study, you open your eyes and look, in diagnosis, you close them and think' (1917, p. 347). Florence Hollis' textbook that was so influential during the 1960s repeats Richmond's advice and warns social workers of the need to distinguish observing from theorising to 'guard against 'contamination' of one with the other' (1966, p. 170). More recently, critics of the way research has been conducted in social work point out that positivist researchers often believed they could be neutral fact-gatherers, collecting information 'in such a way that our fingerprints do not leave any trace on them. In other words, they remain uncontaminated by the gathering process' (Everitt *et al*, 1992, p. 6). Taylor also criticises scientists' claim to objectivity, seeming to believe that it rests on a claim that they theorise from a neutral standpoint rather than on the way their theories are tested: 'I do not accept the myth of researcher objectivity ... and believe that familiarity with the subject matter enhances the research' (1993, p. 129). No physicist or chemist would disagree with her contention that it helps to be familiar with the subject matter.

However, as the student social worker asked to keep records or to write a case study knows, there are no obvious facts to record. There is no clear indication of what is significant and what can be ignored as irrelevant. Scientists do not have an empty mind when they look at the world. They already have some expectations, preconceptions, and questions in their heads. To start with, some decisions have to be made about which facts to collect. In practical terms, collecting *all* the facts is impossible – and undesirable since the resulting mass would be unmanageable. Suppose we wanted to study social work with abusing parents to discover which methods were effective. What limits are there to the data about the clients and about what the social workers did that could be observed? Decisions have to be made about what aspects of the interaction are potentially relevant. Even if we focused on only one social work interview, the range of possible data is virtually infinite. Should we record all that was said and the body language as it was said? How much description of the client and the social worker is needed? Does the ethnic origin of both matter or the colour of their socks? However detailed the description of the interview, it will leave out numerous aspects of the event.

Decisions also have to be made about what sections of time and space need to be examined. The social work interview is a salient aspect of practice but there is no guarantee that all the significant causes will be present in it. David Thorpe criticises research into child abuse for 'context stripping', for failing to study the contexts, the social circumstances, of abusing parents and thereby overlooking significant areas of causation. Thorpe attributes this error to scientific methodology itself, claiming that it requires that 'the subjects of research are decontextualized and objectified' (1994, p. 29). While his criticism may be an accurate comment on the research that has been done, he is wrong to blame it on the scientific approach itself rather than on the choices made by particular researchers.

O'Hear (1989) illustrates this point with the real-life example of doctors studying the high rate of puerperal fever causing many maternal deaths in one particular ward of the Vienna General Hospital between 1844 and 1848. Without success, the doctors examined the women's general condition and their treatment, comparing them with another ward with a much lower incidence of the fever. A male colleague then died of a similar illness after cutting himself on a scalpel that had been used in an autopsy. This made them think of investigating the possibility of a link between autopsies and the fever. They then observed that the women on the affected ward were examined by doctors who had come straight from conducting autopsies without cleaning their hands well. Once they started disinfecting their hands before touching the women, the death rate fell to a tenth of its previous level.

In practice then, scientists cannot approach their subject with an empty mind but have to make some decisions about how to study it, about where to look and what facts are worth collecting. The main criterion is potential causal significance. For example, in studying social work, it seems plausible to suggest that people from different ethnic backgrounds may respond differently to social work help but, offhand, it is difficult to think of how sock colour could affect the progress of the interview. This assumption may be wrong and by omitting to record the colour of the socks, an important correlation may go unnoticed. Similarly, when social workers assess a client, they make decisions about what areas of the client's life are relevant. Their theoretical assumptions will affect this decision. Those with a behaviourist leaning will focus on a significantly different set of facts than those influenced by Freudian theories.

Beside having to decide what facts are relevant in a given area of study, scientists have to decide how to organise them. On the Baconian view of scientific method, scientists note similarities and regularities in the data collected. The decision on whether to class two events as similar or different, however, is not a neutral one. Any two events can be seen as similar in some respects and different in others. Two social work interviews might be the same in that they involved the same people but different in that the topics discussed varied. Deciding which similarities are to form the basis of your categoris-ation of events requires making some assumptions and conjectures about what is going on. For some theories, two events will be alike while for others they would be classed as dissimilar. A behaviourist might class smiling at a child as similar to giving him a sweet because they are both types of reward though there are obviously many differences between the two actions from other points of view. O'Hear makes the point:

Without some presupposition, tacit or explicit, we will not see two events or objects as similar at all.

For if there are respects in which any two events are similar, there will also be respects in which they will be dissimilar. (1989, p. 18)

In social work nowadays, this issue is particularly relevant as management develops information systems for monitoring practice more closely. The interests of senior management and accountants are different from those of practitioners and so their choice of relevant information and useful categories for recording can seem to social workers to create a grossly inaccurate picture of their work. Management may class two child abuse investigations as similar because they took an equal time and both ended with the cases being closed. The social workers involved though might have a completely different view with the cases differing sharply in the ease with which the investigation was carried out and the confidence they have in their final decision. Although the facts collected by a management information system may look neutral, choosing which ones to collect and how to classify them involves making assumptions about the purpose and nature of social work practice.

In summary, the Baconian idea that scientists could observe the world from a neutral position is false. Scientists make assumptions about what to observe and how to organise their observations and these are not determined by the nature of the data themselves but by the scientists' initial speculations about what is possibly relevant and worth studying. There is no guarantee that their assumptions will be correct and lead to fruitful theory development. Until the colleague in the Vienna Hospital died of a similar illness, doctors did not think of looking for a connection between autopsies and puerperal fever. Until there was widespread belief in social work that child sexual abuse did occur, social workers did not notice the evidence that would be considered to raise the possibility of sexual abuse.

THEORIES ARE CONJECTURES

The second faulty element in Baconian philosophy of science is the view that, having collected the facts in a neutral manner, scientists then apply a set of inductive principles to them to discover the underlying scientific laws. With this view of science, the imaginative conjectures of social workers about their clients look radically different from the plodding data collection of scientists. But theories go beyond what has been observed in two ways. First, theories generalise from the limited number of observed instances to all cases, observed and unobserved, future and past. For example, on the basis of observing some gases, scientists theorise about the behaviour of gases in general.

Secondly, and more importantly, science is not simply a matter of reporting correlations between two sets of events but of trying to explain why those correlations occur and this, in most cases, involves speculating about underlying processes. Newton-Smith in his book on current philosophy of science points out that the Baconian picture of scientists just identifying correlations in the world may have had an element of truth in the seventeenth century when such discoveries were an important part of the developing sciences but it is radically inaccurate of modern science: 'the discovery of correlations between observables, far from being the end of science, is but its beginning. Science begins when, having noted correlations, we seek an explanation of why they obtain' (1981, p. 211).

For example, research has shown that children who have been abused are more likely than average to grow up to abuse their own children. This correlation does not satisfy scientific curiosity but sparks it off. Why is there this connection? How does the experience of being abused influence future parenting?

Answering these types of questions usually involves speculating about underlying processes and postulating the existence of unseen entities. Physics in this century has seen 'the development of theories introducing ever more theoretical items and properties for explanatory purposes' (Newton-Smith, 1981, p. 211). The belief that so many social workers have, that scientific methods cannot be applied to studying the mind because it is not directly observable, is misguided. Physicists speculate about sub-atomic processes as behaviourists conjecture about people's learning mechanisms and psychoanalysts hypothesise about subconscious processes.

Scientific theorising as described here bears a strong resemblance to the way social workers try to understand clients and to everyday reasoning about people. The strict behaviourists were exceptional in wanting to reject our commonsense approach. Most philosophers have taken the view that there are many similarities between intuitive reasoning about people's behaviour and the early stages of theorising in science. The differences lie in the way theories are formulated and tested. The dominant view in philosophy has been that our commonsense wisdom and our power of empathy are valuable sources of ideas to help us formulate scientific theories (e.g. Nagel, 1961, Chapter 13; Papineau, 1978, Chapter 4). They can form the base of a scientific study. In the same way, social workers' practice wisdom can be the starting point for theorising about social work practice.

On closer analysis, practice wisdom resembles scientific explanations in many respects. Like scientists, social workers generalise from their experience with individual clients; they try to explain why the problems arose; and they draw on such understanding to make predictions and to plan how to help clients.

Like a scientist, the social worker learning from experience and developing this practice wisdom is making generalisations about clients. This is essential if insights gained from one client can be applied to others. The worker will identify and classify recurring features. Two clients dealing with a serious bereavement may both be considered to show anger. There will be many differences in the details of the way they express their anger but the social worker may judge that their behaviour is similar in the important respect of being an expression of anger. The social worker is not just concerned with noting the correlation between the patients' circumstances and feeling angry but wants to understand why it occurs, to speculate about the causes of the anger. Since the aim of social work is not simply to understand the client but to help, the worker will also be looking for ways of using that understanding to guide practice. This involves making some predictions about the probable course of events and the likely effect of different responses from the social worker. If practice wisdom is a useful tool in social work then it must help the worker understand the client and his problems and offer advice on how to help.

It is clear from child abuse inquiry reports that social workers need to search for causes and to make predictions. In assessing a family, they try to understand why the child is being abused as a first step to considering the risk of future injury and as the basis for planning how the parents can be helped. The reports frequently criticise them for the poverty of their assessments and the vagueness of their planning but clearly identify the necessity of seeking causes and making estimates of what is likely to happen.

Hardiker's research also provides evidence of how

social workers look for causal explanations. In her study of twenty five social work assessments of child care referrals she found that social workers were not just describing the problem but also conjecturing its causes. A typical example Hardiker gives is of a family referred because the mother said she could not cope with her new baby. The social worker's assessment was of 'a classic case of early bonding failure, possibly due to the physical circumstances of the child's birth, plus the mother's low self-esteem, social isolation and stressful marriage' (Hardiker, 1981, p. 95). In another case, the social worker identified many contributory factors to an incident of child abuse: a difficult birth, a stepfather with little experience or knowledge of child rearing, depression and social isolation in the mother, and the mother having been physically abused herself.

In the social enquiry reports studied by Curnock and Hardiker (1979) there was also evidence that the Probation Officers were trying to identify the causes of the criminal behaviour and predict the likely response to different forms of punishment/treatment. The researchers found that the common areas cited as causes of criminality were: the offender's personality; his health; family dynamics; social relationships (friends and at work); the neighbourhood; and economic circumstances. One Probation Officer, for example, thought that the particular family dynamics of a thirteen year old boy contributed to his delinquency:

I think this (marital problem) has some direct bearing on the boy's behaviour because the family situation is one in which conflict is quite apparent; it does not help him feel secure in his family and again he has this problem of finding out his own identity. The parents have unrealistic ambitions for their children. Therefore, he committed this offence along with his mates for reasons of status and group membership. (Curnock and Hardiker, 1979, p. 43)

McDonald's more recent research also shows the influence of theories on Probation Officers' understanding of offenders and reveals the range of views held by officers. Her sample of ten officers in one probation team were asked to complete a proforma on each client on their caseload indicating what factors they saw as associated with the offending behaviour. She found that the officers varied markedly in what factors they saw as relevant: 'some officers viewed their clients' offending behaviour as having been influenced by a number of social and behavioural factors, others tended to select predominantly social factors, and so on' (1994, p. 420).

Like scientists again, social workers are concerned with making predictions on the basis of their understanding. The Probation Officers were involved in predicting whether the offender was likely to re-offend and how serious his crimes might be. Their proposals were based on predictions about the likely beneficial effects of the various options. Where crimes were thought to be the result of specific factors, that were considered amenable to social work help and where the client seemed co-operative, they advocated a Probation Order.

In child care work, predictions also figure prominently. Because of the statutory duty to protect the welfare of the child, social workers have to estimate risk, both of leaving the child with potentially abusive parents and of providing alternative forms of care.

One feature of science that might persuade social workers that their type of understanding is radically different from scientists' is that so many famous theories make universal claims, such as 'all gases expand when heated'. In contrast, when social workers cite something such as family disharmony as a cause of delinquency, they would not claim that 'all unhappy families produce delinquents'. Nor would they claim 'all delinquents come from unhappy families'. The causes social workers cite are not usually seen as necessary or sufficient conditions for producing the problem but as stresses, risk factors, or precipitating variables. They do not determine a specific outcome but only make it more or less probable. If we attempt to formulate the intuitive wisdom of fieldworkers, we are unlikely to find many universal claims but hypotheses of the form 'such and such a factor tends to increase the probability of X occurring' or 'this often causes Y.' While this differentiates social work wisdom from some of the most successful theories in science, it does not mark an absolute disparity. The language of probabilities is as much a feature of the natural sciences as are universal laws. In the field of quantum mechanics, it is debateable whether it could ever be possible to explain sub-atomic articles in any terms other than probabilities.

STRICT BEHAVIOURISM AND THE EXCLUSION OF
THE MIND

As scientific theorizers go beyond what is easily observed, they face difficulties in devising ways of testing their theories. It is quite simple to think of ways of checking the observed correlation between childhood experience of abuse and being an adult abuser but once we start speculating about underlying processes, we can only test them indirectly. The quark, for example, has been postulated by physicists to explain certain observed phenomena but it cannot itself be directly isolated and examined. The theory of quarks is tested by seeing whether it leads to accurate predictions.

The problem of how to test theories about the mind was a major factor on the development of strict behaviourist methodology at the beginning of this century. J.B. Watson, the first behaviourist, saw that his fellow psychologists who were 'introspectionists' had serious difficulties in trying to test their theories. He also saw that others were having success in studying animal behaviour without any reference to what was going on in their minds. Watson therefore took a radical line, arguing against the standard view that psychology was the study of the mind but claiming psychologists should just study behaviour.

According to the prevailing orthodoxy of 'introspectionism', the mind was the focus of psychological study and the main way of studying it was through observing one's own mental processes – through introspection. Plausible though this idea is, it ran into serious difficulties as a scientific discipline.

First, introspection proved to be of very limited use as a method of investigation since, as was soon recognised, many important aspects of our mental processes are unconscious. Nor does it seem that these unconscious operations can be made conscious even by careful inner observation. Marbe's influential study in 1901 (reported in Mandler and Mandler, 1964, p. 143) showed that when he asked his subjects to compare different weights and to report their mental processes as they did so, their efforts at introspection did not directly reveal the process that led to their judgements about the relative weights. Instead, they reported experiencing hesitation, doubt, waiting for an answer, and feeling that the answer had arrived. Marbe concluded that the process of judging was not carried out at a conscious level and introspection alone seemed unable to reveal how it was done.

But behaviourists argued against even a limited role for introspection in psychology. They claimed that the whole method was essentially unscientific. The problem they saw was that, since introspective reports were of private experiences, they could not be checked and verified by others. De Laguna, one of the early behaviourists, asserted that unconscious processes:

> Can not by the very nature of the case be objects of scientific study. For it is an essential condition of scientific investigation of any phenomenon that observations made by one individual shall be verified by others. (1919, p. 297)

Behaviourists also criticised the failure of introspectionists to achieve intersubjective agreement. When people were exposed to the same stimuli, they often described different perceptions but there was no way of deciding between the two reports. When subjective accounts conflicted, rational debate could quickly degenerate into bickering. For all these reasons, behaviourists concluded that introspection was not a scientifically respectable method of observation.

Watson's solution to the problems of intropsectionism was extreme. Having decided that it was difficult to study mental phenomena, he decided not to study them at all but to concentrate on phenomena that were more readily accessible to reliable and inter-subjectively verifiable observations, namely behaviour. His approach was stricter than general behaviourism because, while he shared their view that only behaviour not mental states could count as empirical evidence in science, he also excluded the concept of mind from theories entirely.

Watson turned to the natural sciences for guidance on methodology but he looked, not at physics where scientists were speculating about unseen processes, but at the study of animal behaviour. He was impressed by researchers such as Edward Thorndike who had made considerable progress in understanding animal learning without reference to any mental experiences they might have.

Thorndike appeared to be producing adequate explanations referring only to observable features of the animal's behaviour and its environment. Extending this behavioural approach to the study of people was, Watson decided, the way to develop a successful science of psychology. The behaviourism he advocated aimed, he said:

> To apply to the experimental study of man the same kind of procedure and the same language of description that many research men had found useful for so many years in the study of animals lower than man. We believed then, as we do now, that man is an animal different from other animals only in the types of behaviour he displays. (1924, p. 2)

Watson's exclusion of mind was even more radical. He claimed not just that one could not investigate the mind scientifically nor did one need to in order to explain human behaviour, but he also doubted that the mind existed: 'the behaviourist holds that belief in the existence of consciousness goes back to the ancient days of superstition and magic' (Watson, 1924, p. 2).

Even within behaviourism, Watson's radical exclusion of all speculation about mental processes was soon challenged as it seemed to obstruct scientific progress. As early as 1932, Tolman argued that, to provide a satisfactory explanation, it was necessary to introduce the concept of the 'intervening variable', something which occurred in the individual between the observed stimulus and the behavioural response. Tolman argued, in line with the natural sciences, that this did not need to be directly perceptible – and so could be a mental process – as long as hypotheses containing it implied observable results. Recent developments in cognitive psychology have moved most psychologists even further from Watson's extreme position. Many found that explanations in terms only of behavioural or physiological responses were inadequate in many areas of behaviour. They therefore turned their attention to studying the role people's thoughts and feelings have in determining their response to stimuli. Their responses are seen as active interpretations of what they perceive. The importance of cognitive factors is also acknowledged in the related therapeutic techniques. Cognitive-behavioural treatments are as concerned with people's beliefs and emotions as with their behaviour and physiology.

The strict behavioural approach however has survived and is more rather than less strongly promoted in social work by some advocates. They value it though not because of any false belief that it offers the only way of studying people scientifically but because the therapies it has produced – behavioural modification techniques – appear from evaluative studies to be very effective in altering elements of behaviour. It is their therapeutic effectiveness that attracts support.

FREE WILL AND CAUSAL EXPLANATIONS

People are generally thought to have free will: an ability to choose what to do and to initiate a course of action. Such an idea of freedom is implicit in our commonsense understanding of people's actions but some social workers fear that it conflicts with a scientific approach that looks for causal explanations. There is no particular difficulty in thinking of our bodies as part of a causally determined physical world. We can accept that our liver and kidneys function according to natural laws. Problems arise though when we consider our thoughts and intentional actions. We generally feel that we have some freedom in choosing how to act; we can deliberate and make a decision but we feel that we *could have* taken another course of action. If all our actions are fully determined by antecedent conditions however, then they are the only ones we could have taken and it is difficult to see how we *could have* done otherwise.

Most of the social science theories taught to social workers are determinist but it passes unnoticed in some while arousing strong objections in others. In psycho-analytic theories, determinism appears to cause few problems for social workers. In behavioural theories, it provokes many criticisms and is cited as yet another reason for avoiding this inhuman approach. Determinism, it is claimed, radically conflicts with our belief in free will, implying that people are 'puppets' (Downie and Telfer, 1980, p. 129), 'slaves' and 'victims' (Perlman, 1965), and 'plastic' (Howe, 1987, p. 29).

The free will/determinism debate is one of the classic problems of philosophy. The belief that we are free agents seems to be challenged by any thesis which implies that our actions are pre-ordained. The problem arose in the ancient Greek culture which had the concept of 'Moira' or 'fate' – the idea that all our behaviour was the inexorable working out of our destiny. This seemed to leave no scope for people to shape their own histories leading the Stoic philosophers to the gloomy conclusion that: 'each of us is assigned a role to play in the tragedy of life ... and there is nothing for us to do but say our prescribed lines as best we can' (quoted in Dennett, 1984, p. 2).

Christian theologians have also been troubled by the problem. They argued that if God, being omniscient, knows everything that has or will happen, then all our future actions are already fixed; the results of our apparently free deliberations are already known to God. Nowadays the success of the natural sciences in developing causal explanations is the major source of doubt over the existence of free will.

There are three main positions on the issue, echoing

the views on the nature of a social science: (a) libertarianism: we have free will in a sense that implies that our actions are not determined; (b) hard determinism: all actions are determined and our familiar sense of freedom is illusory (this position is adopted with relish by some behaviourists who claim that all our behaviour can be understood in terms of environmental factors); and (c) the view that I think offers the most convincing answer: compatibilism: our notions of freedom and determinism can be reconciled.

The compatibilist view has a long history. The eighteenth century Scottish philosopher, David Hume, provided a detailed account of it. Other proponents have been Thomas Hobbes (1651, Chapter 21), John Stuart Mill (1867), A.J. Ayer (1976), and D. Dennett (1984). The basis of their account is to challenge the claim that when we say we made a free choice we mean that we could have done something else in exactly the same circumstances. We feel free, they suggest, when our own wishes and feelings influence what we do as opposed to times when our movements are wholly caused by outside factors. If our hand moves because we intend to wave goodbye, we are acting freely, whereas the sufferer from Parkinson's disease finds that his hand moves whether he wills it or not. Any action though is fully determined by the combination of external factors and our own desires and choices. For a free agent to choose A instead of B, some factor, perhaps a feeling or a wish, must be different to tip the balance and lead to a different action. An agent could not have done something else in *identical* circumstances.

The main philosophical attack on compatibilism is that its account of freedom is unsatisfactory. Critics claim that on such a view of freedom, our sense of being responsible for our actions is illusory. Actions may be caused by 'our' decisions but since, according to determinism, these are themselves determined by external factors the individual could not have chosen any alternative course of action. The compatibilist's defence is that these critics underestimate the significance of the contribution human mental processes make to the causal sequence. Dennett (1984) offers an interesting evolutionary explanation of our ability to be in charge of what we do. At an earlier evolutionary stage, it might have been true to describe man's predecessors as wholly determined by their environment but, as we have acquired rationality and language, we have become increasingly capable not just of reacting but of interacting with the world around them. Therefore we are now, even at birth, capable of complex interaction with our environment. We are not completely self-made but we can claim a significant share of the responsibility. The human agent is an element in a causal chain but such a major one that he has a clear identity.

While libertarians are not satisfied with this account of the human self, their own attempts to define self has been the weakest part of their position. They need the concept of an agent who is more than the sum of his thoughts, feelings, memories, etc. They claim that there is an 'I' who can stand back from my reasoning and make a free decision so that even though all the circumstances, including my reasoning, are identical, I might choose one of several options. But what kind of entity is this? Hume, writing in the eighteenth century, commented on its elusiveness:

> For my part, when I enter most intimately into what I call *myself*, I always stumble on some particular perception or other, of heat or cold, light or shade, love or hatred, pain or pleasure. I never can catch *myself* at any time without a perception, and can never observe anything but the perception. (Hume, 1739, p. 413)

A sense of coercion is common in the criticisms social
workers aim at determinism. They use emotional images
of 'slaves', 'puppets', and 'victims'. But in what sense does
determinism imply such duress?

The philosopher Daniel O'Connor (1971) offers a
plausible explanation of this fear of being constrained. He
suggests that a major cause of hostility to determinism
arises from confusing causation and coercion. The laws of
Parliament are prescriptive, permitting certain behaviour
and forbidding deviations under pain of punishment. The
laws of nature are descriptive, telling us what does
happen. With respect to Parliamentary laws it is meaning-
ful to talk of coercion, but not with the laws of nature. It
is misleading to imagine a causal law as some kind of
slavemaster, whipping us into line if we try to do anything
on our own initiative. The planets are not compelled to
follow the orbits assigned to them by relativity theory
while secretly yearning to deviate along different paths.

In ordinary usage we say we are coerced when we are
made to do things by external factors despite our wishes
and, in such cases, our actions are not thought of as free.
This distinction between forced and free actions is pre-
served by determinism, as O'Connor says:

> To say that my conduct is free is merely to say that it
> is under my own control. And it is under my own
> control if it is guided by my own intentions, motives,
> and desires. But to say this is certainly not to say that
> my conduct is in any way UNCAUSED. (1971, p. 74)

Another possible source of the slave and victim imagery
is the fear that, if our actions are determined then, in
principle, they are predictable. This can create a fear that
we might be controlled, not by causal laws, but by an
intelligent being. And, from the metaphors chosen by
social workers, the fear seems to be that this could be an

evil rather than a loving being -evil scientists (probably behaviourists) who use their knowledge of causal laws to control and manipulate us to their own ends.

Dennett (1984) notes how common this nightmare is in the literature on free will. But, surprisingly, there is considerable agreement on the question of predictability between libertarians, compatibilists *and* hard determinists. Even the libertarians accept that some prediction is possible since they concede that our behaviour is often subject to regularities. The complexity of human behaviour however is generally thought to rule out precise prediction. The behaviourist Skinner (1974) says such prediction is impossible, likening the complexity of behaviour to that of a rainstorm. While physicists can make some predictions about the general pattern of its behaviour, they would be unable to predict with confidence the exact trajectories of each droplet of water.

Dennett argues that our rationality adds another layer of complexity to prediction. Since we are relatively intelligent and reflective beings, we do not have a simple consistent response to experiences but actively appraise them. We can examine incoming information rationally, judge its truth in the light of our past experiences, decide whether it suits our goals, etc. And to confound anyone trying to predict our reaction even further, we may, feeling stubborn, bored or frivolous, act to alter our response from what was expected. We do not just receive information but process it in a highly personal way and it is this which makes the final use of information 'our choice'.

In contrast to social workers' fears of being controlled by an omniscient scientist, the social sciences tend to produce only explanations in terms of probabilities and, as far as both libertarians and determinists can see, this is all we are likely to achieve.

Determinism worries many people because it seems to

threaten our familiar and valued sense of being responsible decision-makers, in control of our actions and our
destinies. It is only if you think of rational human beings
as, in fact, very simple reactive organisms that these fears
look plausible. Once you acknowledge the complexity of
our thinking, determinism does not threaten the belief
that 'I' make decisions about what 'I' should do. The
people who need social work help suffer from many social
disadvantages. Their freedom of action is threatened from
many directions, by poverty, illness, or prejudice, but not
by social workers' acceptance of determinism.

OBSTACLES TO DEVELOPING THEORIES
The resemblance between social work and scientific reasoning seems strong. Both are concerned with understanding their subject area by forming generalisations,
looking for causes, and making predictions. There are
however aspects of current practice which complicates the
task of theory development.

Unfortunately, though I am presenting science as the
desirable model and arguing that there are no insuperable
barriers to developing practice wisdom into explicit theories, science offers us no simple, mechanical way of
doing so. Theories are not the product of some computer
scan of sets of data but the imaginative creations of
scientists trying to work out why the data is as it is. Social
workers wanting to formulate their ideas into explicit
theories will have to show a similar level of imagination
and intelligence. It takes time and effort to articulate
one's thoughts. If social workers are to formulate their
background reasoning in more detail, they need encouragement and work conditions that allow them to spend
time on this intellectual process. Social workers can and
do reach decisions intuitively without listing the whole
process by which they reached that conclusion. Under the

pressures of a busy caseload, it is quicker to proceed to act on those decisions than to try to explicate their assumptions and their reasons. They can draw on theories without being conscious of precisely what theory a particular idea came from. In the short term, working intuitively is swifter and cheaper.

The quality of social workers' implicit reasoning can also be an obstacle to articulating it. Woolly thinking cannot be formulated as clear theories. There is evidence from several sources indicating that many social workers do not work from a clear assessment and plan, implicit or explicit, but react as problems are presented by clients. Goldberg and Stevenson's research studies discussed in Chapter One both reported the tendency of workers not to have clear goals and plans. Vernon and Fruin's (1986) research on social work with children in care bears out their findings that social workers often have incomplete assessments, unclear plans, and make little review of progress. Many of the abuse inquiries also illustrate a standard of reasoning that few would defend as adequate, regardless of their views on the art/science debate. Secker's (1993) analysis of how students developed during their training provides a valuable insight into how social workers may vary markedly in their ability to formulate their reasoning. Her third category, of the 'fluent' approach, was only achieved by a few students but is a far better starting point for formulating practice wisdom than the other two types. Students in this group were able to integrate both commonsense wisdom and theories in their work with clients. They showed a higher awareness of what theories they were using and could examine them critically. They were also much more able than the other two categories to say what they were doing and why. They were able to share their thinking with clients and with supervisors. In the current social work culture where the personal nature of practice wisdom gives individuals a high degree of privacy in their work, it is hard to detect poor standards of practice.

Formulating practice wisdom is also complicated by the varied theoretical base of social work. The degree of personal selection apparent in social work training leads to a set of practitioners who each have their own knowledge base which may have more or less in common with their colleagues. To express their thinking in a public language they need a shared terminology. While there will always be scope for some variation of theoretical approach in social work, the present scenario in which variation proliferates produces problems for developing a clear agreed language for describing social work.

If we look back to a time when there was greater agreement on the theoretical base, at least among trained social workers, we see that it coincided with a greater willingness and ability to formulate practice and share it with colleagues. In the 1950s and 1960s, the psychosocial approach based on analytic theories was dominant on social work courses. In the specialisms of psychiatric social work and medical social work where qualification was a necessary requirement, there was considerable consensus on the appropriate knowledge base. Their journals reflected this in having regular columns where some-one presented a case and it was analyzed and discussed in subsequent editions.

The degree of variety in knowledge base has made the task of drawing up guidelines and procedures more difficult. The Department of Health (1988), for example, has tried to improve the range and quality of social work assessments by producing a guide to social workers in child abuse cases 'undertaking a comprehensive assessment'. The guide does not make its theoretical base explicit but states it covers all 'relevant' areas. As the earlier discussion in this chapter showed, facts cannot be collected from a theory-neutral standpoint. The guide has had to make assumptions and decisions about what areas are relevant but there is no indication of the basis for these decisions. From the point of view of some theories, social workers following the guide would not collect all the relevant evidence and make a comprehensive assessment as intended. For a behaviourist, for instance, there would be insufficient detail of the circumstances surrounding times when the child was chastised or rewarded. On the other hand, someone using a psychoanalytic theory of personality development would want a substantially different set of information. The attempt to formulate practice wisdom will need to go hand in hand with the development of shared language for describing and categorising social work reasoning and the knowledge base on which it is based.

CONCLUSION

At present, social workers rely mainly on practice wisdom that, because of its individual and private nature, cannot be evaluated in detail by the standard procedures of science. Critics of a scientific approach say that this state of affairs cannot be altered, that practice wisdom cannot be expressed as scientific theories. They suggest a striking contrast between social work and scientific reasoning. On the one hand, social workers regard their clients as rational, purposive people with free will and try to understand what is going on in their minds by using empathy and imagination. On the other hand, scientists are depicted as strict behaviourists who focus exclusively on behaviour, ignoring mental processes.

The tendency to equate science with behaviourism is to some extent understandable because, within social work, so many advocates of a scientific approach also propose behaviourism and behaviourism exemplifies a narrow, and in important respects faulty, view of science that is held by many non-scientists. Behaviourism however is not representative of science. It adopts a narrower methodology than other disciplines. The more accurate account of science I have described does not look significantly different from social work reasoning at least in the area of developing theories. There are strong similarities in the way scientists theorise and social workers reason about their clients as they build up practice wisdom. Both are making a conjecture about the causal processes behind the phenomena they want to explain. Theories do not grow out of observations in any mechanical way. They are not considered reliable because of the way they are built up from the facts but because they are subsequently tested empirically. A theory is a conjecture, an imaginative leap beyond the data involving speculation about the processes underlying the evidence that has been observed.

There seems no inherent obstacle to making practice wisdom explicit but, unfortunately, science offers no mechanical system for formulating theories and, like scientists, social workers will need intelligence and imagination to devise testable theories. The current, personal style of practice in which diversity of theoretical base proliferates and where woolly thinking can go undetected makes the task harder.

The crucial difference between scientists and social workers lies not in how they theorise but in how they test their ideas. Science provides methods for testing theories empirically which can provide a more reliable test than the intuitive and empathic judgements of social workers.

CHAPTER 6
Reliable Evidence

Scientists test theories by deducing predictions about the world from them and then, through experiment, checking whether those predictions are true or false, that is, whether the world conforms to the picture predicted by the theory. If a psychologist predicts, on the basis of learning theory, that a person with arachnaphobia will be able to handle spiders without anxiety after going through a behaviour modification programme, we can test this by checking that the phobic has received the specified therapy and then watching what affect spiders have. If the person still runs away at the sight of a spider, the prediction has been falsified and this casts doubt on the claims made for learning theory.

Empirical evidence can support or refute a theory because it is independent of the theory and publicly accessible. We can all see, for example, whether the phobic starts sweating and runs away at the sight of a spider or whether he can handle it in a relaxed manner. What counts as empirical, however, has been a major philosophical issue and revolves around theories of meaning. Empirical evidence takes the form of *statements* about observations, not observations themselves. Scientific rea-

soning, whether deductive or inductive, involves relationships between sets of statements, not between statements
(theories) on the one hand and experience on the other.

Social workers are familiar with the claim that only
descriptions of behaviour constitute acceptable evidence
in science; they provide 'hard' facts. Reports about mental
states and processes, what people think and feel, are said
to be non-empirical and so inadmissible as scientific
evidence. The demand for behavioural evidence creates a
gulf between social workers' ordinary ways of working
and the scientific model and has undoubtedly contributed
to their hostility to science. But this distinction stems
from the positivists' theory of meaning about observation
statements which has been shown to have serious faults.
Its rejection has led to a sweeping reassessment of how to
obtain reliable evidence in the social sciences. The purpose of this chapter is to explain why the positivists'
theory of meaning is faulty, to discuss alternatives, and to
illustrate how scientific criteria for evidence can be used
in social work practice and research.

THEORIES OF MEANING AND REFERENCE
In science, there is an important distinction between
theoretical and observation terms. While, as will be seen,
there are debates about this distinction, it is easy, at an
intuitive level, to understand the difference. Compare, for
example, the two statements: 'this child has blue eyes'
and 'this child is suffering from maternal deprivation'. To
describe eyes as blue is to refer to a property we can
check uncontroversially by direct observation. Moreover,
if several of us look at the child, we can usually agree
whether or not the eyes are blue. This is classed as an
observation statement.

Statements about maternal deprivation are not so easy
to test. Many people will not know what it means. To
understand the term requires some knowledge of the

psychological theory in which it occurs. To decide whether or not a child is maternally deprived is a difficult process and one which, in the current state of development of the theory, is likely to be controversial. Terms like this are classed as 'theoretical'. The theory of maternal deprivation can be tested by deducing predictions from it, by specifying, for instance, how you expect the separation from the mother to show up in the child's future conduct.

Positivists thought that the distinction between theoretical and observation terms was a difference in kind, not just in degree, and that the different types of terms got their meaning in different ways. They held a correspondence theory of meaning for observation terms. The leading positivist, Carnap (1953, p. 367), defined observation terms as those that *correspond* to an observable quality whose presence or absence can be established in a relatively short time and with a high degree of agreement. The concept of 'blue', for instance, would meet this definition. By contrast, a holistic theory of meaning was proposed for theoretical terms. They were considered not to refer to objects or processes in the world but to take their meaning from their position within the network of concepts in a theory. 'The concepts of science are the knots in a network of systematic interrelationships in which laws and theoretical principles are the threads' (Hempel, 1966, p. 94).

In the social sciences, this absolute distinction between observation and theoretical statements was reflected in the sharp distinction between behavioural and psychological terms. Psychological terms were held to refer to non-observable properties or processes in the mind. They were therefore classified as theoretical. Behavioural terms, on the other hand, were deemed observable and so could provide the empirical base for the social sciences. What someone does, rather than what he believes, hopes or feels, was said to provide what the philosopher Ernest Nagel (1961) called the 'competent' evidence for testing theories.

But the positivists' claim that observation statements could be verified by experience alone has not stood up to scrutiny. On closer analysis, they turn out to go beyond what can be known on the basis of immediate experience. To use the philosopher Karl Popper's example, the statement 'here is a glass of water' is checked by experience – by looking – but also by using terms such as 'glass' and 'water' which involve many assumptions: 'by the word "glass", for example, we denote physical bodies which denote a certain law-like behaviour, and the same holds for the word "water"' (Popper, 1959, Chapter Five).

It might be argued that observation terms can be distinguished from theoretical on the grounds that the former can be ostensively defined. That is, we can point to objects in the world and say 'that is blue', 'those are eyes', but not 'that child is maternally deprived'. However, although there seems to be a significant difference here, it is a matter of degree not of kind. As Polanyi (1967) has shown, even learning an ostensively defined term requires making some unverifiable assumptions. If we take the concept of 'blue' as an example, we can teach someone what blue means by pointing at various blue objects. However we are pointing at the objects as well as the blueness and the learner has to conjecture which common property is being referred to. Telling him it is the colour we are picking out will only help of he already understands the concept of colour and, to have learned this, he will have needed to make some theoretical assumptions.

If all observation statements presuppose some theoretical assumptions, then they cannot get their meaning just from corresponding with the world and they are not direct, infallible reports of experience. The underlying

assumptions can be rejected or modified and, consequently, a statement once accepted as true may be
rejected. The foundations of science are not as firm and
neutral as positivists thought.

This conclusion is generally accepted but its implications are controversial. Empiricists treat it as a 'weak
thesis': that all terms involve some presuppositions but
there is still a category of observation terms which get
some of their meaning from their reference to objects in
the world. These form a common ground between rival
scientific theories that can provide the neutral territory in
which theories can be tested. Hence, behaviourists and
psychoanalysts will disagree at the theoretical level of the
causes of a fear of spiders but agree at the level of saying
'this man is sweating' or 'this is a spider'.

The 'strong thesis' however, adopted by relativists, is
the claim that there is no evidence that can provide an
independent test of theories; all observations are said to
be permeated by the theory for which they are used as
evidence. Criticisms of this strong thesis are discussed in
more detail in Chapter Eight as part of a critique of
relativists' view of science in general.

The empiricist recognises that all observation reports
involve some assumptions but does not accept the relativists' claim that they must assume the very theory being
tested. Behaviourists and psychoanalysts have some presuppositions in judging that 'this man is sweating' but
they are common to both groups and separate from their
rival psychological theories about why he is sweating.

The rejection of a sharp distinction between observations and theoretical terms, however, does have significant implications for the social sciences. There are no
longer grounds for saying that reports about behaviour
are different in kind from psychological descriptions. All
involve going beyond what is given directly in experience.
It might be argued that there tends to be a higher rate of

agreement in using behavioural terms. There is unlikely
to be much dispute, for instance, in judging whether a
child has blue or brown eyes. Describing people's mental
state is, however, often controversial. But one can think
of examples where there is higher agreement about the
person's mental state than some aspect of their behaviour.
It may be obvious to everyone, for instance, that someone
is feeling furious but there might be dispute about
whether his cheek muscle was twitching.

It must be remembered that, in ordinary language,
many terms are vague and imprecise, particularly in
comparison with terms in science, and in this respect,
psychological language is not exceptional. Colour is often
cited as a paradigm example of an observable property
but, in general speech, there are many disputes about the
use of colour predicates. There is considerable agreement
on what counts as a primary colour such as blue or red
but there is ample scope for argument when it comes to
shades like turquoise, violet, or amber. These colour
concepts have much vaguer, varied rules of use.

Colour concepts can be given a precise and consistent
meaning and the way this can be done illustrates two
important aspects of how scientists develop a clear and
shared use of language. Each colour can be defined by
reference to wavelength. This is possible because scientists have developed an extensive theory about colours
which allows them to give any shade a precise description
in terms of wavelength. They have also developed instru-
ments which enable them to measure wavelengths accurately. The gradual refinement of concepts in science
usually goes hand-in-hand with theory development.

The differences apparent in ordinary usage between
behavioural and psychological terms, then, are a matter
of degree not of kind. Moreover, intuitive, everyday
concepts, whether behavioural or psychological, typically
need to be made more precise to standardise usage for

scientific purposes. Developing a shared use of language is an important task in social work not just for research purposes but to improve communication between social workers and others. The next two sections look at the strategies proposed by positivists for eliminating psychological language: the 'reducibility' thesis and 'operational definitions'. They deserve attention because they contain useful ideas on making concepts more precise though both have subsequently been discredited in their pure form.

LIMITS OF THE REDUCIBILITY THESIS

The reducibility thesis claims that psychological language can be reduced to behavioural terms, that is, we can specify the criteria for using the psychological term by reference only to directly observable features of the environment and people's behaviour. We can reduce, say, the concept of sadness to descriptions of certain types of behaviour in certain circumstances. The thesis has some plausibility if we consider the way we learn to understand and use psychological language. A boy learning the concept of anger, for instance, does so by hearing the word used by others in a variety of settings. He needs to work out the rules for when it is appropriate to describe someone as angry and, for this to be possible, he must be able to observe some differences between the contexts in which it is used and those where it is not. He will notice, for example, that it is often associated with loud voices and critical comments and less often with laughter and smiles. He will also learn to link it with his own experiences – he will learn when to describe his emotion as anger. Carnap expounded the thesis:

> There cannot be a term in the psychological language, taken as an intersubjective language for mutual communication, which designates a kind of

state or event without any behaviouristic symptom. Therefore there is a behaviouristic method of determination for any term of the psychological language. Hence every such term is reducible to those of the thing-language. (1975, p. 371)

Tolman, a behavioural psychologist, provides an illustration of this thesis in practice. He offers a definition of 'the rat expects food at location L' in non-psychological terms:

> When we assert that a rat expects food at location L, what we assert is that *if* (1) he is deprived of food, (2) he has been trained on path P, (3) he is now put on path P, (4) path P is now blocked, and (5) there are other paths which lead away from path P, one of which points directly to location L, *then* he will run down the path which points directly to location L. (in Taylor, 1964, p. 79)

The reducibility thesis has been attacked on the grounds that it is not feasible in practice (Putnam, 1978; Scriven, in Krimmerman,1975, Chapter 32; Taylor, 1964). These critics agree that behaviour and environment are important factors in our reasoning about other minds and learning to use psychological language. It is the *complexity* of our rules for using mental terms that is seen as the stumbling block.

We can show this by returning to Tolman's attempted reduction of 'expect'. He has specified the kind of behaviour which would indicate that the rat expected to find food at location L but his account is not completely equivalent to what we generally mean by 'expect'. If, for example, the rat went to the path that went to L but, before he could run down it, someone picked him up, on Tolman's account he can no longer be described as expecting to find food. In ordinary usage, however, we would still say that he expected food but that the unexpected factor of being picked up prevented him from finding it. Tolman could also accommodate it by adding the proviso: 'and if he is not picked up' to his original definition. The problem to critics of the reducibility thesis is that there are so many of these factors which we can allow for in ordinary language that the behaviourist cannot hope to spell them all out in advance. It is therefore unrealistic to try to implement the thesis.

Behaviourists seem to endorse this point. Zurriff, in his overview of behaviourism, having explained why behaviourists deny that any reference to psychological states can be classed as observational, goes on to comment:

> Nevertheless, in practice, most behaviourists use action language almost exclusively in describing behaviour. Action-neutral descriptions of behaviour are difficult to formulate, and action language is therefore used for convenience. There is a trade-off between observational purity and usefulness. (1990, p. 42)

The central idea of the reducibility thesis – explaining complex concepts by reference to simpler terms – has always been valued, in everyday life as well as in science. We use this strategy to define terms to each other or to clarify how we reached a particular judgement. When social workers make an intuitive judgement about a client, it does not appear from nowhere. It has crystallised from what they have seen and heard, their feelings about the client, and the theories they hold about human nature. They are often not wholly conscious of how they have reached their judgement but they can, with some intellectual effort, analyse their reasoning and bring it out into the open. At a child protection case conference, for

instance, the social worker who wants to convince sceptical colleagues that the family is making progress can give
examples of the type of evidence that has led to that
judgement – that the child has been attending school
regularly, the baby has been seen at the clinic each week
and is gaining weight satisfactorily, etc. But, when taken
to the positivists' extreme of trying to reduce all psychological language to behavioural terms, the reducibility
thesis is unwieldy, as well as unnecessary, in practice.

MEASUREMENT THEORIES NOT OPERATIONAL
DEFINITIONS

The other strategy of positivists for dealing with psychological language is to define them operationally. Most of
the older textbooks on research for social workers tell
them to provide operational definitions of their concepts
(e.g. Tripodi, 1983, p. 44).

Bridgeman (1927) provides an early and classic account
of this approach. The central idea is that the meaning of
every theoretical term must be specified by prescribing a
definite testing operation that provides a criterion for its
application. For example, 'intelligence' could be operationally defined as the score obtained under specific
conditions on a specific I.Q. test. Operationalism, as
originally set out by Bridgeman, maintains that the meaning of a term is fully and exclusively defined by its
operational definition:

> The concept of length is therefore fixed when the
> operations by which length is measured are fixed:
> that is, the concept of length involves *as much as and
> nothing more* than the set of operations by which
> length is determined. In general, *we mean by a
> concept nothing more than a set of operations;* the
> concept is synonymous with the corresponding set of
> operations. (Bridgeman, 1927, p. 5, my emphasis)

While it is agreed that we need ways of measuring concepts, the claim that the ways of measuring provide a full definition has been comprehensively criticised. It would rule out the possibility that one term can be measured in several different ways. For instance, if we define the *length* of an object in terms of measuring it against a standard, rigid, measuring stick then we cannot use this concept of length to refer to the length of the circumference of a cylinder since it cannot be measured by a rigid stick. Since we need to specify a new way of measuring the cylinder, we are defining a new concept of length, according to operationalists. This is contrary to the commonsense view that the concept of length is the same in both cases but Bridgeman claims that common-sense is wrong.

Hempel (1966, p. 123) points out that scientists do not share Bridgeman's view that each way of measuring refers to a different concept. He also argues that if they adopted this form of operationalism, it would hinder scientific development. Scientists treat two procedures as measuring the same property if they are consistent in the sense that, in areas where both are applicable, they produce the same results. Physical theory assumes one concept of length and many, more or less accurate, ways of measuring it. The criteria for measuring a concept are not treated as definitions. A definition is stipulative; it states what meaning you are assigning to a term. Scientists treat operational criteria as empirical; on this view, they are fallible and subject to review and modification. They are more appropriately called observation or measurement theories than definitions.

This distinction between definitions and theories is more than a linguistic quibble. Definitions can be specified by researchers – for instance, 'by "cohesive family" I mean a score above fifty on the family cohesion question-naire' – and, to a great extent, others have to accept the definition. When the testing procedures are seen as theories, however, they are seen as open to critical review. The researcher is not claiming to define the term but to propose a way of measuring it. Others may question how satisfactory a measure it is.

In the current state of affairs, social workers are more likely to want to criticise the measurement theories of management than of researchers. Responding to the increased demand for accountability, managers have developed criteria for measuring the quantity and quality of service provision. For many social workers, practice now includes the tasks of completing forms and compiling statistics. Whether these are a good measure of the key features of good practice is debatable.

RELIABILITY AND VALIDITY

In judging a measurement theory, the two key concepts are validity and reliability. Validity is defined by Reid and Smith (1989, p. 199) as 'the extent to which a measure corresponds to the "true" position of a person or object on the characteristic being measured ... it attempts to capture an elusive property of measurement: its truth value'. How valid, for example, are the official employment statistics as a measure of the level of unemployment in this country? Validity cannot be ascertained beyond doubt; it 'is inevitably a matter of judgement based on evidence and inference'.

Reliability is an aspect of validity which is treated separately because it can be assessed reasonably precisely. It refers to the extent to which observations or measurements are consistent over time and between observers, whether, for instance, a blood pressure test produces similar results when repeated on the same patient whose blood pressure has not altered, or when used by different doctors. The main methods of judging reliability are test-re-test consistency and inter-rater agreement (Reid and Smith, 1989, p. 199).

The criticisms of positivist social work research can be rephrased in terms of these criteria. Researchers have used behavioural indicators because they tend to have higher reliability, that is, inter-user agreement, but they are criticised for having low validity, being often only a marginal measure of the concept being studied. Similarly, problems with management information systems can be expressed in the same way. In order to obtain reliable data, measurement or recording is made of features of practice where it is easy to get inter-user agreement, for instance, in noting when a referral was received and when it was closed. Obtaining a more valid measure would entail considerable work in developing shared rules for using more complex concepts such as aspects of good quality practice.

It is possible to improve the inter-user rate, or to develop a clearer, shared meaning of a term. We learn shared meanings in ordinary life just through talking and social workers have developed their own words for describing some aspects of practice. It is also possible to improve agreement by following, to some extent, the principles of the reducibility thesis and operational definitions.

The research project on high expressed emotion as a factor in relapse rates of schizophrenia provides an excellent example of how usage can be standardised. From clinical experience and research on relapse rates for schizophrenia, it seemed plausible that patients who returned to live with families in which there was high expressed emotion were more likely to suffer a relapse than those in families with low levels of expressed emotion.

In a series of studies, Brown *et al* (1962, and 1972), and

Vaughn and Leff (1976), evidence for the causal significance of levels of expressed emotion was accumulated
and the concept itself increasingly refined. To test their
hypothesis, the research team trained observers to use
this complex concept of expressed emotion with very high
inter-user agreement. The way this was done is interesting
both because it reveals the complexity of the task and
because it uses a combination of analysis and user skill.

Researchers being trained to use the concept are told
not only how to rate expressed emotion but are given
guidance on how to collect the relevant information. In
two methodological papers, Rutter and Brown (1966) and
Brown and Rutter (1966), a detailed description is given
of (a) the most appropriate techniques of interviewing,
describing a style which encourages respondents to
develop their own lines of thought rather than being
guided too much by the interviewer, (b) a semi-structured
interview schedule, listing the areas in which information
is sought, and (c) the criteria for rating expressed
emotion. This final category is broken down into five
measurements: of the level of critical remarks, degree of
emotional over-involvement, hostility, warmth, and positive remarks. The last measurement, of positive remarks,
is made simply by counting the number in an interview of
a specified length. The others are measured in a more
subjective way but, nevertheless, consistently. People are
trained to measure them by being given examples of the
types of comments which would indicate high or low
levels but, unlike the positivists' operational definitions,
no attempt is made to spell out the full procedure for
rating expressed emotions; the interviewer's new skill in
applying the concept is an essential component. To
achieve consistency in use, training uses case examples
and videos to standardise judgements. The research team
report that, with this training, they are able to get very

high inter-user agreement on rating expressed emotion (Berkowitz *et al*, 1981).

Another empirical study well known to social workers illustrates how researchers can study people' subjective experience. Brown and Harris (1978) investigated the social causes of depression in women. Earlier research had implicated what was imprecisely called 'life events' in the causation of depression. Methods had been worked out for interviewing people and rating their 'life event score' in a consistent way. Brown and Harris, however, thought that a major defect in earlier rating systems was that they had not considered the 'meaning' of the life event to the individual; they had treated: 'a wide range of events as alike that are not alike. The birth of a child does not mean the same thing for all women' (Brown and Harris, 1978, p. 81). They therefore decided that the existing scheme of rating life events was inappropriate:

Incidents once classified as 'events' were treated as equivalent as far as severity of threat, disruption, and the like were concerned. We now needed in some way to bring meaning back. (1978, p. 85)

The interviewing schedule was changed to find out not only whether life events had occurred but the woman's response to them: 'in the sense of the thoughts and feelings she had before, at the time, and after the event' (1978, p. 86). Each interview was tape-recorded and the tapes later used to complete 28 rating scales covering each event. These were then used to 'make a judgement about the likely meaning of the event for the average person in such circumstances' (1978, p. 90). To avoid bias, the raters did not know whether or not the women had developed depression after experiencing the life event.

Studies such as these not only show how researchers

can refute their critics' claims that they only study behaviour but also suggest ways that social workers can develop a better, shared use of language in talking about their practice.

EVIDENCE IN SOCIAL WORK PRACTICE

The concepts of reliability and validity are also useful for social workers in their daily practice as they consider the value of the evidence they have for their judgements. Social workers make judgements throughout their contact with a client or family: the initial assessment of their problems, the goals of their intervention, judging the progress of the case, and deciding when to close the case. In adopting a more open and critical style of practice, they need to clarify how they reach these judgements so that they, and others, can consider the accuracy and reliability of their evidence.

Under the pressures of a busy caseload, social workers cannot hope to achieve the standards of researchers but analysis of child abuse inquiry reports (Munro, 1996) illustrates some of the most common errors social workers tend to make in appraising evidence. While these reports only deal with child care cases, the type of practice described fits the picture of the other research cited in Chapter Two.

Department of Health guidelines (DoH, 1992) and textbooks stress the importance of differentiating 'fact' from 'opinion' but this overlooks the need to question whether the 'fact' is true or not. Social workers need to consider where they have learned the fact and whether this is an accurate or trustworthy source.

Inaccuracy can creep in just through the process of communicating the fact. People make mistakes when writing up records or noting down a phone message; they misunderstand what someone says to them. Fallibility of this kind is a probably inevitable feature of social work practice. It can have serious repercussions. Forty percent of inquiries noted an error in communication that went undetected and which was judged to have adversely affected the way the case was then dealt with. Heidi Koseda and Stephen Meurs both died of starvation but, in each case, social workers' concern about them had been allayed by mistakenly believing they had been seen alive and well by a health visitor (the health visitor *had* called but not seen the child). Accurate information might have led to more urgent efforts to see the children and their poor state of health would have been immediately obvious. Doreen Aston's health visitor told her social worker that she was losing weight but it was recorded as 'baby gaining weight and growing' (Area Review Committee, Lambeth, Lewisham and Southwark Boroughs, 1989). The doctor examining Richard Clark at the social worker's request mistakenly thought the referral was about chicken pox not physical abuse (HMSO, 1975a).

The high rate of serious miscommunications found in inquiry reports suggests that it is prudent for social workers to check details which carry a lot of weight in their appraisal of a case.

Facts can also be inaccurate because people are dishonest. Parents can tell lies about their child's injuries; neighbours and relatives can make malicious allegations. Even when not being deliberately dishonest, people tend to be biassed in judging what seems significant and worth reporting. Neighbours who dislike a family find it easier to think of examples of their faults than their virtues.

Inquiry reports show the lengths abusive parents will go to hide the truth and how persuasive they can be. When Charlene Salt had broken ribs, her parents told social workers they were going on holiday and then hid from sight until the injuries were undetectable. Jasmine Beckford's parents went to considerable efforts to stage-manage the social worker's visit to hide the fact that

Jasmine could not stand properly because she had a broken leg. Sukina's parents waited each time for the bruising to fade before taking her for medical treatment and kept going to different hospitals so that professionals did not realise the frequency or severity of her injuries.

In contrast to the examples of parents deceiving social workers, other members of the public had trouble in being believed. Many child abuse referrals come from relatives or neighbours who have seen injuries or who are worried about the general level of the child's care. Since the public inquiries deal, on the whole, with cases where children were actually abused they provide a biassed sample so it is not surprising they contain examples of true, not malicious, allegations from members of the public. Since we do not know how many allegations from neighbours are false, it may be that social workers are right, in general, to be very sceptical about them but what the reports reveal is that social workers do not investigate these referrals as thoroughly as referrals received from professionals. They were markedly less likely to call a case conference to obtain a wider picture of the family, and were more likely to reject allegations, out of hand, as false. The reports repeatedly criticise them for deciding to reject neighbours' or relatives' allegations on inadequate evidence.

Social workers were also frequently criticised for being content with a very imprecise way of measuring some factor. Maria Colwell's social worker thought Maria was gaining weight after she returned home but this was based on a visual appraisal. She was in fact steadily losing weight, an ominous sign that would have been picked up if the social worker had checked the weight by using scales (HMSO, 1974). Malcolm Page was taken into care because of the poor standard of care of the children and the house. When he returned home, the social worker judged the state of the house by looking at one room only. The bedroom where Malcolm died was in an appalling state (Essex County Council, 1981).

Besides considering the accuracy of the evidence, social workers need to consider the *range* of information they have. We would not expect a pollster estimating the population's political opinions to ask only one or two people for their views and, in a similar way, we should not make a broad judgement about a family's functioning, for example, on the basis of one or two observations. For this reason, collaboration with other professionals is important since they see families in a number of different settings. Many of the recurrent criticisms in inquiries, however, relate to the narrow range of information social workers collected about a family.

Overconfidence' in one's judgements is a recurrent finding in social psychology research (Kahneman et al, 1990, Part IV). It also appears repeatedly in inquiry reports in that social workers show a tendency to treat their intuitive judgements as reliable and to see no need to crosscheck them.

Intuitive appraisals of individuals or families were often accepted without question or review even if based on just one short interview. One family interview lessened the social worker's concerns about Kimberley Carlile (London Borough of Greenwich, 1987) so he did not call a case conference or treat further investigation as urgent. He was criticised by the inquiry for not checking his appraisal of the family. There was plenty of information available at the time to challenge such an optimistic assessment of family functioning.

Neil Howlett's care was strongly influenced by the social worker's judgement at the first interview that his brother was a scapegoat and that Neil was not at risk because he was more important to his mother than his brother. The brother was taken into care but Neil stayed with his mother who killed him four months later. The inquiry comment on how this false initial judgement was picked up by other workers and accepted without question, a confidence the inquiry found strange since many of the concerns the professionals had about the family centred on the welfare of Neil not his brother (Birmingham City Council, 1976).

Overconfidence in her initial judgement was also displayed by Leanne White's social worker. After investigating the first allegations of abuse, she decided there were no grounds for concern. When she received allegations from two other sets of neighbours, she did not reconsider her judgement but ignored the referrals (Nottinghamshire Area Child Protection Committee, 1994).

Social workers tended to limit the range of their evidence by concentrating on the present and overlooking past behaviour. This was evident in the eight cases where they were criticised for failing to read their own records. This allowed major items of information to go unnoticed – such as the fact that the children were on the 'at risk' register (HMSO, 1980). John Aukland's new social worker was happy to accept John's benign account of the death of his first child without looking in the records which would have told him that John had been convicted of manslaughter and sent to prison for his daughter's death (HMSO, 1975b).

Even the information the current social worker had acquired was liable to be forgotten. The social worker closely involved with the family can be distracted by current events and drift away from the original assessment of risk and protection plan with serious consequences. Tyra Henry was on a Care Order because her father was violent to children. While he was in prison, Tyra was adequately cared for by her mother and grandmother and the social worker was reassured about Tyra's welfare so that, when the father came out of prison, she continued to consider that there was little cause for concern (London Borough of Lambeth, 1987). In another case, Maria Colwell was taken into care because of neglect but when she returned home her social worker was reassured by the absence of signs of physical abuse and did not specifically monitor for neglect although there was growing evidence of it (HMSO, 1974).

The picture of social work practice portrayed in inquiry reports and other studies of practice is of practitioners relying heavily on their intuitive and empathic skills. Reasoning is often left unarticulated making it hard for the social worker or others to say on what evidence they are basing their judgements and, consequently, making it difficult to scrutinise its accuracy. Clearly listing the evidence and asking some basic, simple questions about its reliability would reduce the number of errors in social work practice.

CONCLUSION

Social workers can only move towards a more public, accountable body of knowledge by using language. They need to formulate their thinking about clients in words and those words need to have a clear, shared meaning both to communicate their ideas unambiguously to others and to allow them to be tested. This raises the key issues of how language gets its meaning and how it can be made more precise.

The positivists' theories of meaning led to their claim that only behavioural reports could provide empirical evidence. This influential philosophy had a pervasive influence in social work. In research, it restricted the type of studies carried out. Many now think that researchers were avoiding the subjects of most importance to practitioners because of the methodological difficulties they posed. To social work practitioners, the positivist philosophy helped to broaden the gap between their way of thinking about clients and what was seen as the scientific way to study people.

The sharp distinction between psychological and behavioural language collapses along with the correspondence theory of meaning for observation statements. Observation and theoretical terms are now seen as on a continuum rather than belonging to two separate categories. This has led to a liberalisation of research methodology with researchers trying to develop reliable and valid measures of concepts without trying to meet the onerous requirement of eliminating all reference to psychological terms. While the positivists' suggestions on how to eliminate psychological language – the reducibility thesis and operational definitions – have serious defects in their pure form, they nevertheless have value in that they offer ideas on how complex concepts and judgements can be analyzed and how usage of terms can be standardised.

In daily practice, social workers can also make use of the concepts of reliability and validity in judging the evidence they have for their judgements about clients. Questioning the accuracy and the range of their evidence will help to reduce errors of the type repeatedly found in inquiries into child abuse deaths.

Evidence, however, does not have a simple relationship with a theory. We now need to turn to the issue of how to weigh the evidence and how to use it to make a judgement about the truth or probability of a theory.

CHAPTER 7

Weighing the Evidence

How should social workers use the evidence to judge a theory or hypothesis? The question has received surprisingly little discussion in the social work literature. Textbooks and manuals give lists of what evidence is relevant in a particular area but offer little guidance on how to weigh it. Yet, as this chapter will show, it is a complicated issue that has been the subject of considerable controversy and debate in philosophy.

Social workers need to judge theories at both a macro and micro level. In their training, they are presented with a wide range of conflicting theories and need to make decisions about which ones, if any, they should use in their fieldwork. Would a psychoanalytic approach to helping a depressed mother be better than a behavioural one? Should her problems be interpreted in the context of the social pressures and constraints under which she lives? Their appraisal of theories should also be reviewed as social workers gain experience of applying them or new research evidence is published. On a daily basis, social workers also have to make judgements about their current assessments of clients and the effectiveness of their ways of helping. As work progresses, new infor-

mation is gained about a client and social workers need
to judge whether this fits their existing views or casts
doubt on them.

In relation to reviewing theories, scientific standards
vary radically from those used in everyday life. The
sixteenth century philosopher of science Francis Bacon
noted how reluctant people are to change their minds.
Once the human mind has formed an opinion:

> It draws all things else to support and agree with it.
> And though there be a greater number and weight of
> instances to be found on the other side, yet these it
> either neglects or despises, or else by some distinc-
> tion sets aside and rejects. (1620, p. xlvi)

Modern psychology research provides considerable evidence to support Bacon's claim. Summing up the findings
of research on this, Nisbett and Ross conclude:

> People have few of the formal scientist's skeptical or
> disconfirmatory skills. Once formulated or adopted,
> theories and beliefs tend to persist, despite an array
> of evidence that should invalidate or even reverse
> them. (1980, p. 10)

Kahneman's more recent survey of the literature reaches
a similar conclusion:

> It appears that beliefs – from relatively narrow
> personal impressions to broader social theories – are
> remarkably resilient in the face of empirical chal-
> lenges that seem logically devastating. (1990, p. 144)

Analysis of child abuse inquiry reports shows that social
workers are vulnerable to these human errors. Many of
the recurrent criticisms of social workers relate to their

failure to review and revise their judgements (Munro, 1996). Once an optimistic assessment of the parents was formed, it was maintained despite growing evidence of risk to the child. Stephanie Fox's social worker continued to believe her parents had stopped abusing her despite forty episodes of bruising (Wandsworth Area Child Protection Committee, 1990). 'The overall attitude that comes through to the inquiry is one of fixed attitudes' commented the inquiry into the death of Karl McGoldrick (Northern Regional Health Authority, 1989). Social workers can be equally slow to revise a judgement when it is critical. The Cleveland inquiry into the sudden and dramatic rise in diagnoses of child sexual abuse criticised the paediatricians and the social workers for persistently failing to consider that the diagnoses might be wrong so that any evidence that conflicted was discounted or re-interpreted so that it was consistent with their judgement that the children were being abused (HMSO, 1988).

In the cases subject to inquiries, social workers' judgements about risk of abuse correlated strongly with the quality of their investigations and monitoring. Inquiries recognise that social workers have to make decisions on the basis of imperfect knowledge and the death of a child does not show that any professional acted incompetently. Forty-two percent of the inquiry reports expressly stated that the social workers had acted reasonably and, in some cases, to a high standard (Munro, 1994). When abuse was suspected but there was insufficient evidence to warrant removing the child, social workers were often praised for the quality of their monitoring and investigation, searching diligently for supportive evidence and checking information that conflicted with their view. Conversely, when they had decided an allegation of abuse was unsubstantiated, they accepted supportive evidence without question and were very sceptical about any new evidence suggesting risk to the children, often rejecting it without checking further. For example, in the case of Leanne White (Nottinghamshire Area Child Protection Committee, 1994) the social worker investigated the first allegations from neighbours but, having decided they were unfounded, dismissed complaints from other neighbours out of hand without even taking a note of their names and interviewing them herself.

Leanne White's social worker acted as if her initial assessment that Leanne was not at risk was true. If it were true, then it would logically imply that the neighbours' allegations were false and no further investigation would be needed. But social workers, like scientists, cannot rationally achieve such certainty. Evidence can support but not prove a theory.

THE PROBLEMS OF INDUCTION

In social work, science, and daily life, we usually assume that past experience is a guide to the future. Social workers develop practice wisdom on the basis that their experience with past clients can be usefully applied to work with future ones, or that a client's former behaviour is a guide to future conduct. This is inductive reasoning. It raises philosophical questions about its reliability and justification.

The problem of its reliability is illustrated by Bertrand Russell's famous but sad tale of the turkey. Every morning, the farmer went to the run to feed his flock. The turkey noticed this regularity and, reasoning inductively, began to look forward to the farmer's visits and would run out to meet him, expecting food. But one day, just before Christmas, the farmer changed his routine and, instead of giving food, picked the turkey up and killed him instead. Inductive reasoning can lead to a false conclusion.

The problem with inductive arguments is that the evidence for our theory or belief is never conclusive. The *general* conclusion is reached on the basis of our limited experience of *particular* instances. A theory about *all* planetary movements, for example, is supported by observations of relatively few planets. But how can we be sure that our generalisation is true, that it will still hold when applied to hitherto unobserved planets or to the same planets at some future date? The answer is that we cannot know with certainty. Other forces that we do not know about may be at work, such as the farmer's business plans, that alter the course of behaviour.

Since inductive arguments can be wrong, scientists can never prove with certainty that a theory is true. To test a theory, scientists deduce empirical consequences and then carry out research to find out whether those predictions are accurate or not. If they are accurate, they provide inductive support for the theory; if they are false, they cast doubt on the theory. But however much inductive support is accumulated, it is always logically possible that the theory is false. The simple generalisation 'all swans are white' received substantial support over many centuries but, when explorers reached Australia, they discovered black swans and falsified the generalisation.

Although inductive arguments cannot guarantee the truth of their conclusions, most of us would still accept that they provide the best method of reasoning beyond our experience, of generalising our beliefs to similar phenomena we have not directly observed or to future events. The turkey was certainly disappointed by the change in the farmer's behaviour but, since he did not know the farmer was only fattening him up for market, his expectation of being fed was, on his past experience, reasonable but wrong. Social workers, too, reason inductively when, for example, they assess a family and predict whether a child is at risk of being abused. It is, in fact, difficult to imagine what we would do if we did not accept that the past was a guide to the future (and if the world

did not behave in a way consistent with that assumption).
We could not, for example, learn language if we did not
expect people to use words in a fairly consistent way.

It has proven difficult, however, to justify inductive
reasoning. David Hume, an eighteenth century philosopher, provides the most famous discussion of this point.
The most obvious justification of induction is that it
works; it may be wrong sometimes but, on the whole, it
produces fairly reliable ideas. But Hume (1739) pointed
out that this type of argument is circular: the past success
of induction is being used as evidence for its future
reliability when what we have been asked to justify is
exactly that principle of using the past as a guide to the
future.

Despite many philosophical efforts, the problem of
justifying induction has never been solved to everyone's
satisfaction. Hume, though, did not see his criticisms as
undermining our use of induction. In his view, we cannot
help believing in a physical world and reasoning inductively about it. Scientists, in general, follow this approach,
accepting that a theory can never be conclusively proved
but thinking that it can be judged more or less probable
in the light of the empirical evidence.

For social workers who are hostile to science, doubts
about induction are not usually among the reasons for
their antipathy. Indeed, induction plays as much a part in
a humanist approach to understanding clients since it is
assumed that social workers can learn from experience
and develop practice wisdom to use in future work.

JUDGING THE PROBABILITY OF THEORIES

Scientific theories cannot be proven but, with the exception of Karl Popper whose philosophy is discussed later,
philosophers and scientists accept that evidence provides
grounds for increasing confidence in a theory. Social
workers who consider that play therapy helps children

who have been sexually abused will have their belief strengthened if they provide the therapy and see the expected improvement in the children. But how much increased confidence should they have and how many instances of failure should they see before they should doubt the value of the therapy? These issues have been the centre of philosophical debate: how to measure the degree of support evidence provides and, linked to this, how to decide between rival theories.

This chapter offers the Bayesian account which holds that 'scientific reasoning is reasoning in accordance with the calculus of probability' (Howson and Urbach, 1989, p. 12). Not only does this account avoid difficulties met by rival accounts but it presents the issues in language that is easily linked to the way social workers reason intuitively. It has plausibility because it captures the way scientists talk about their reasoning. Dorling (1979, p. 180) reports that it is rare to find any scientist in the last three hundred years who does not talk in terms of probability. The Bayesian approach also has the attractive feature of providing a uniform account of the universal theories more commonly found in the natural sciences and the probabilistic theories that predominate in the social sciences.

The account is named after Thomas Bayes, an eighteenth century clergyman, who derived the central theorem which works out how much more or less probable a theory is in the light of a new piece of evidence. The new probability is based on three factors: the theory's previous probability, how strongly the theory predicts the evidence, and how likely the evidence was, given background knowledge alone even if we did not hold the theory.

The first factor – the 'prior probability' – is the most contentious aspect of the Bayesian account of scientific reasoning but also one which closely resembles current social work practice. It is the scientist's subjective appraisal of the plausibility of the theory given background knowledge of the subject area. This subjective element is unwelcome to many who want to provide a wholly objective account of science but Howson and Urbach argue that it is, in practice, an unavoidable aspect of science: 'scientists always discriminate, in advance of any experimentation, between theories they regard as more or less credible and so worthy of attention (1989, p. 80). Calculating the prior probability involves a subjective judgement in the sense that individuals with different knowledge, beliefs or backgrounds may assess it quite differently. Social workers calculate prior probabilities when they judge theories or evaluate their practice subjectively. The Bayesian approach does not require them to abandon this custom but to treat it as a first step in a more rigorous appraisal.

The second factor in Bayes theorem is how strongly the theory predicts the evidence, that is, if the theory is true how probable is it that the evidence will be found. A deterministic theory such as 'all gases expand when heated' predicts with certainty that, if this is a gas and has been heated, then it will expand. So the probability of the evidence equals 1. If the prediction is wrong, then the theory is falsified. Most theories in the social sciences are stated only in terms of probabilities so that a particular finding has only some degree of likelihood. Being abused as a child is thought to increase the probability of abusing one's own children but knowing that a father had been abused would not lead a social worker to predict with certainty that he would be an abusive parent; it would make it more likely.

The third factor is the likelihood of the evidence given background knowledge alone. The degree of support a finding gives a theory depends on how much more likely it is given the theory than it is on background knowledge alone. This reflects the value scientists give to surprising predictions. Howson and Urbach (1989, p. 86) argue that this intuition is true in everyday experience as well. They give the example of a soothsayer. If he predicts that you will meet a dark stranger sometime and you do so, your confidence in his predictive powers will not be much increased since meeting a dark stranger is almost inevitable if you live in Britain. If, however, the soothsayer were to predict the correct number of hairs on the head of that stranger, you would be amazed and your scepticism would be shaken because, without the hypothesis that the soothsayer can foretell the future, making such a correct prediction is highly improbable.

In Bayes theorem, the 'posterior probability' – the revised probability of the theory in the light of the new evidence – is calculated on the basis of these probabilities. Howson and Urbach (1989) provide the following formal version of Bayes theorem, if t stands for theory and e for evidence:

$$P(t/e) = \frac{P(t)}{P(t) + \dfrac{P(e/\text{not } t)\, P(\text{not } t)}{P(e/t)}}$$

Having spoken only of the merits of a Bayesian approach, let me turn to its critics. Bayes theorem itself is not controversial. The axioms from which it is derived are common to most accounts of probability. The main criticism levelled at the Bayesian approach concerns its subjective element: fixing the prior probability of a theory is said to be a subjective decision by a scientist. In this respect, this philosophy fails to meet the hopes of objectivists like Popper, Lakatos, Carnap and, in statistics, Fisher, Neyman and Pearson who all want an account of science in which to use Lakatos's words: 'the cognitive value of a theory has nothing to do with its psychological influence on people's minds' (1978, vol.1, p. 1).

On this point, Howson and Urbach have two main defences of Bayesianism: first, the failure of their opponents to develop an adequate objective method of assigning prior probabilities, and, secondly, the failure of their critics to take account of how limited the subjective element is.

The rival probability approach has tried to establish the objective probabilities of theories, using only factual data and the logical structure of the hypotheses – and *no opinions*. The assumption is that, if two people have the same factual data, they should assign the same prior probabilities. Theoretical views or personal factors should have no influence on the computing of probabilities. Howson and Urbach (1989, Chapter 3) argue that not only have the objectivists failed in their task but also failure is unavoidable. Purely objective criteria for determining prior probabilities do not exist; all methods must make some assumptions about the data:

> No prior probability or probability-density distribution expresses merely the available factual data; it inevitably expresses some sort of opinion about the possibilities consistent with the data. (1989, p. 289)

The seekers after objectivity fear that, if prior probabilities are assigned in part subjectively then Bayesian reasoning is: 'a record merely of the whims of individual psychology' (Howson and Urbach, 1989, p. 289). This, argue Howson and Urbach, is to greatly overestimate the significance of the subjective element. While the individual decides the initial probabilities, what happens to them subsequently is determined by the probability calculus. They suggest the analogy with deductive logic. This does not tell us whether the premises of our argument are true or false but, once we have decided their truth-value by independent means, it dictates the valid inferences we can make from them. Similarly, Bayesian theory does not tell us the prior probabilities of our ideas but, once these have been given a particular value, it computes their posterior probability. 'As far as the canons of inference are concerned, neither logic [neither inductive nor deductive] allows freedom to individual discretion: both are quite impersonal and objective' (1989, p. 290).

One might expect that the subjective element would lead to radical variations in the assessment of the probability of a particular theory in science and this seems counter to experience. Natural scientists generally reach a high degree of agreement on the merits of their theories. However, applying Bayes theorem, major disagreements do not usually last for long because, when weighed against a common body of evidence, the posterior probabilities typically converge rapidly as evidence accumulates. A low prior probability will be substantially increased by empirical evidence while a high one will only be affected slightly. Therefore, after a few tests have been done, most of the initial difference will have disappeared.

A social work example will help to illustrate how the Bayesian approach works in practice. Let us suppose that we face the common problem at a case conference of deciding how much a new piece of information about a family increases the chances that the child will be abused. For example, they may have heard that the child was a premature baby and had a low birth weight. The new calculation of risk uses three probabilities: a current estimate of the risk to the child, how common the new factor is among abusing families, and how common it is in the population in general.

First the prior probability, how likely the claim that the parents will abuse the child is on existing knowledge before adding the new evidence. All those at a case conference have some view about whether the child is at risk or not though there may well not be agreement. The implications of their differing opinions will become apparent in the next few pages.

The second probability measures the probability of the risk factor among abusers. Premature birth and low birth weight are known to be predictive of abuse but how strongly do they predict it? Few social workers will be able to answer this. The guidelines provided by most local authorities list risk factors but give them no weighting. Browne and Saqi (1989, p. 68) quote research evidence that 24.2 per cent of abused children were premature and/ or had low birth weight.

The third probability measures how likely it is that the evidence will be found in the general population, whether or not they abuse their children. Again this information is not generally given to social workers in their guidelines but Browne and Saqi (1989, p. 68) provide a figure of 3.2 per cent. for premature birth and/or low birth weight.

We can now show the impact of this new evidence and how it has different effects depending on how much at risk the child was thought to be. Let us suppose that the social worker was very concerned about the child and so thought the prior probability of abuse was high and estimated it at 0.8. Using the other statistics quoted above, the new probability, the posterior probability, =

$$\frac{0.8}{0.8 + \underline{0.03 \times 0.2}} = 0.97$$
$$0.24$$

But suppose, as often happens, some-one else at the case conference had a very different view of the family. Perhaps the GP thought the parents were coping well and estimates the risk at a low figure such as 0.2. The calculation is now:

$$\frac{0.2}{0.2 + \dfrac{0.03 \times 0.8}{0.24}} = 0.67$$

The social worker and GP still differ in their estimation of risk but their estimates have moved much closer together. The new evidence has more impact on the low estimate because it is much more unusual to find low birth weight in non-abusing families than in abusing ones.

The importance of knowing how common the factor is both in abusers and in general can be further illustrated by looking at an example where the incidence of the risk factor is not much higher than average in abusing families. Suppose the case conference has been told not about low birth weight but that the child is physically or mentally handicapped, a factor which might be thought to add to the stress on the parents and therefore make abuse more likely. The statistics in Browne and Saqi (1989, p. 68) are that this factor appears in 1.6 per cent of abusing families and 0.8 per cent of the general population. The social worker's new estimate of risk would be:

$$\frac{0.8}{0.8 + \dfrac{0.008 \times 0.2}{0.016}} = 0.89$$

The GP's new estimate would be:

$$\frac{0.2}{0.2 + \dfrac{0.008 \times 0.8}{0.016}} = 0.3$$

Because the factor is only slightly associated with abuse and is only a little more common among abusers, it does

not have a dramatic impact on the estimates of risk. Both
have increased slightly but there is still a big discrepancy
between the social worker and the GP.

Scientists do not sit down with pocket calculators to
work out the probabilities of their theories nor would I
suggest that case conferences adopt such a formal habit.
But it is important for them to understand the central
features of the calculation. The importance of the new
evidence depends on two factors: how often it appears in
abusing families and how often it appears in the population. A piece of evidence may be very rare among abusers,
such as a spiral fracture of the humerus, but if it is almost
unknown outside abusing families then it is highly predictive of abuse. Equally something may commonly be found
among abusers, such as being aged in their twenties, but
if this is an equally common finding among all parents of
small children, it has little predictive value. The more
surprising the new information if the family are not
abusers, the more its occurrence increases the chance that
they are abusers.

Scientists often discuss their theories in terms of probabilities. Evidence cannot prove a theory with complete
certainty but it can make it more or less probable. The
Bayesian approach which bases scientific reasoning on the
probability calculus offers a coherent account of inductive
reasoning which captures the generally accepted features
of scientific judgements.

REFUTATIONS: POPPER'S ACCOUNT
Falsifications play a major role in scientific reasoning. The
claim that 'all swans are white' cannot be proven beyond
all doubt by any number of white swans but it can be
refuted by finding one black swan. There has been
agreement among philosophers for centuries about the
importance of falsifications but Karl Popper is famous for
making it the centre of his account of scientific method.

Scientists, he says, are not trying to prove theories but to disprove them. He claims that scientists do not use fallible inductive reasoning in appraising theories but deductive reasoning based on falsifications. His work is well known and has been proposed as a model for social workers (Sheldon, 1978, Gambrill, 1990). However, his philosophy has been the subject of such damaging criticisms and offers such an inaccurate account of scientific methods that it should not be held up to social workers as a model of the way they should judge theories. Examining its defects also helps to clarify the process of scientific reasoning.

Popper's interest in the philosophy of science was fuelled by his experience as a social worker in Alfred Adler's child guidance clinics in Vienna. He reports that many of his friends had enthusiastically embraced psychoanalytic theories but Popper became worried by what he saw as their uncritical acceptance of them. They interpreted *all* evidence as confirming the theory; nothing seemed to count against it. The study of psychoanalysis:

Seemed to have the effect of an intellectual conversion or revelation, opening your eyes to a new truth hidden from those not yet initiated. Once your eyes were thus opened, you saw [apparent] confirming instances everywhere: the world was full of [apparent] *verifications* of the theory. Whatever happened always confirmed it. (Popper, 1963, p. 34)

Popper writes that he was spurred into studying philosophy to try to understand how science differed from this, as he saw it, dogmatic approach. He reached his well-known conclusion that the hallmark of a scientific theory is that it is falsifiable. While there is general agreement that refutations play a central role in science and that the apparent verifications seen by enthusiastic psychoanalysts do not really support the theory, his account of science as a whole has been severely criticised.

Let me begin with a brief account of his philosophy before detailing the main objections. Popper makes the point that, with inductive reasoning, we cannot prove a scientific theory is true beyond doubt but, because of the asymmetry between positive and negative results, he claims that we can know with certainty that a theory is false. Although finding hundreds of white swans never conclusively proves the hypothesis 'all swans are white', discovering one black swan disproves it.

Popper makes the extreme claim that not only can evidence not prove a theory but also it cannot increase its probability. Scientific theories, Popper says, can never be inductively supported only deductively falsified:

> The method of falsification presupposes no inductive inference, but only the tautological transformations of deductive logic whose validity is not in dispute. (Popper, 1959, p. 42)

When scientists draw out the empirical consequences of their theories and design experiments to test them, according to Popper, they are not trying to confirm their theories but to disprove them. They do not prefer one theory because it seems more probable or better supported by the evidence but because it has so far withstood their attempts to falsify it.

Where inductivists describe positive results as 'supporting' a theory, Popper talks of 'corroboration'. This sounds similar but has a substantially different meaning. Popper's 'corroboration' carries no implication of increased probability. Indeed he claims that the theory remains a highly improbable conjecture but, by withstanding attempts at refutation, it shows its 'fitness to survive'. To call a theory well-corroborated is to report on its past performance not to make any prediction about its future merits. If it were seen as an indicator of its future performance, this would involve inductive reasoning which Popper is trying to exclude completely from science.

This account of science has received a very critical response from his fellow philosophers. First, Popper claims that one certain feature of science is that an observation statement that conflicts with a prediction from a theory can falsify that theory with certainty. Yet Popper agrees with the point discussed in Chapter Six that observation statements are not infallible; direct reports of experience can be wrong. If it is logically possible that the observation is wrong then it is logically possible that the theory, although apparently falsified by it, is true. The alleged objective certainty is, in fact, illusory.

In practice, scientists sometimes query the results rather than accepting them as counter-evidence. Newton is reputed to have done so when the Astronomer-Royal reported observations which conflicted with Newton's own theories; on repeating the observations, the Astronomer-Royal found he had made a mistake. Newton's reluctance to accept these apparent refutations was, therefore, justified.

Another criticism of Popper's methodology is that it is not the way scientists actually work. They do reason inductively and talk of theories being more or less probable. At best, he is prescribing what scientists *ought* to do, not describing what they are doing. This option, though, is also criticised. Putnam (1974) raises an objection that seems particularly relevant to social workers. Popper's attempt to exclude induction, he argues, is based on an unreal picture of science. To Popper, scientists are only interested in knowledge for its own sake whereas, Putnam points out, science is about developing knowledge that can be *used*. Therefore, scientists must be concerned about the future reliability of their theories, not just their past performance. So inductive reasoning is an unavoidable part of any practical science:

> When a scientist accepts a law, he is recommending to other men that they rely on it – rely on it, often, in practical contexts. Only by wrenching science altogether out of the context in which it really arises – the context of men trying to change and control the world – can Popper even put forward his peculiar view on induction. Ideas are not *just* ideas; they are guides to action. (Putnam, 1974, p. 335)

Social workers use theories as guides for action. Accepting a theory affects what they do and has major repercussions for clients, possibly leading to a child being removed from his parents, or an offender being recommended for a custodial sentence instead of a probation order. Social workers have to make predictions; they have to decide which hypothesis is more plausible, trustworthy or probable. As Putnam asserts:

> Since the application of scientific laws does involve the anticipation of future successes, Popper is not right in maintaining that induction is unnecessary. Even if scientists do not actively anticipate the future (and of course they do), men who apply scientific laws and theories do so. (1980, p. 335)

Another major problem for Popper's philosophy is the Duhem-Quine thesis. Duhem (1905) and Quine (1953) both pointed out that experiments in science involve more than a single conjecture and an empirical observation. To derive a prediction, additional premises are needed, at least to state that the initial conditions, are met, i.e. that the circumstances to which the conjecture refers are present. In the simple example of the hypothesis 'all swans are white', we need an additional premise that 'this is a swan' before we can infer 'this is white'. If observation shows that this swan is black, we may conclude that the *set* of premises as a whole is false but logic alone does not tell us which premise is wrong. On investigation, we might conclude that the bird had been wrongly classified as a swan so that his colour would not falsify the generalisation.

Falsification, then, does not hit a specific hypothesis. When a prediction is proved wrong, scientists have to make some change in the premises but no particular one is logically targeted by the refutation. Consequently, as Quine emphasised;

> Any statement can be held to be true come what may, if we make drastic enough adjustments elsewhere in the system ... Conversely, by the same token, no statement is immune to revision. (1953, p. 43)

In fact, scientific theories are rarely as simple as the swan example and so a falsified prediction usually contradicts a far bigger set of premises than just two, complicating still more the question of which premise is at fault. Indeed, as the philosophers Lakatos (1970) and Kuhn (1970) have highlighted, predictions in science are typically derived from several theories. Lakatos describes scientists as working within a 'scientific research programme', such as psychoanalysis or behaviourism. The research programme is a unit consisting of a so-called 'hard core', the central theories such as Newton's laws, and a 'protective belt', comprising the auxiliary theories which are needed to link the hard core to empirical observations. The latter are described as protective because, when faced with falsifying evidence, scientists will generally revise them rather than the central theories. Kuhn, whose philosophy is examined in more detail in the next chapter, has a similar concept of 'paradigm'.

When we apply Popper's ideas on falsification to a research programme or a paradigm, we run into serious difficulties.

Popper claimed that scientific theories, unlike non-scientific theories, were falsifiable, a point echoed by Malcolm Payne in his social work textbook (1991, p. 44). However Lakatos and Kuhn make the point that some of the most highly valued scientific theories would be classed as unscientific by this criterion because, on their own, they are untestable: 'exactly the most admired scientific theories simply fail to forbid any observable state of affairs' (Lakatos, 1970, p. 100).

Putnam illustrates this with Newton's theory of universal gravitation. This is a law which specifies the force every body exerts on every other body, but:

This theory does not imply a single basic sentence! Indeed, any motions whatsoever are compatible with this theory, since the theory says nothing about what forces other than gravitations may be present. The (gravitational) forces are not themselves directly measurable; consequently not a single *prediction* can be deduced from the theory. (1974, p. 358)

Testing such an abstract theory only becomes possible when it is connected with lower level theories. In Lakatos' terms, it forms part of the hard core of the Newtonian research programme. While the research programme is progressive or the paradigm is successful, scientists assume the truth of the central theories; any falsifications are seen as not challenging them. Refutations are dealt with either by altering one of the lower level theories or merely leaving it to one side as an anomaly while the more fruitful aspects of the theory are explored.

This version of how scientists treat the most highly valued theories is a serious challenge to Popper's account of science. In the face of these criticisms, Popper gave up his initial claim that theories can be judged scientific by seeing whether they are logically falsifiable. He modified his position to the claim that scientists should treat their theories as falsifiable. They could do this, he suggested, by being willing to state in advance what evidence will make them give up a theory:

> *Criteria of refutation* have to be laid down before-hand: it must be agreed which observable situations, if actually observed, mean that the theory is refuted. (1963, p. 38)

Returning to Popper's original goal of demarcating science from what he considered to be the pseudoscience of psychoanalysis, he claims that psychoanalysts are not scientific because they are not willing to propose any such criteria:

> What kind of clinical responses would refute to the satisfaction of the analyst not merely a particular diagnosis but psychoanalysis itself? (1963, p. 38, foot-note 3)

The trouble, for Popper, is that this does not differentiate psychoanalysts from natural scientists. Lakatos points out that it is just as true of Newtonians:

> But what kind of observation would refute to the satisfaction of the Newtonian not merely a particular version but Newtonian theory itself? (1970, p. 101).

Refutations do play an important part in scientific appraisal of theories but Popper fails to provide a feasible account of either what scientists currently do or what they should do.

REFUTATIONS; THE BAYESIAN ACCOUNT

Popper raises an important issue when he expresses concern about his psychoanalytic friends seeing 'confirming instances everywhere . . . whatever happened always confirmed it'. There does indeed seem something wrong if any findings whatsoever can be cited as support for a theory. A similar concern motivates Brian Sheldon when he encourages social workers to use only theories that are falsifiable. Social workers, he complains, make little effort to find refutations and, if some are found, they fail to take them seriously as a challenge to their ideas. They use 'theories containing built-in defences against disbelief' (Sheldon, 1978, p. 14) so that any apparent refutation can be accommodated. Sheldon claims, too, that social workers have such vague goals that virtually any outcome can be interpreted as favourable. He cites the case of Mary, a schoolgirl known to a particular Social Services Department, who was expelled from school. On the face of it, this is an undesirable event, suggesting that current social work efforts to help had not yet succeeded. Her social worker, however, did not see it in a negative light. Expulsion from school was, Sheldon complains, 'massaged into "a not altogether unwelcome opportunity to re-evaluate Mary's educational options"' (1978, p. 583).

Something does indeed seem wrong, as Sheldon says, if social workers can interpret any result as positive. Popper's discussion, however, gives the impression that, to inductivists, these confirmations give genuine added support to a theory. But this is not so and the Bayesian approach can explain why.

The degree of support evidence provides is based on

three factors, one of which is the finding's improbability given background knowledge alone. If it is just as probable whether or not we hold the hypothesis, then it offers no support. If a particular finding is predicted by the theory but is otherwise highly unlikely then it provides strong confirmation.

Suppose, for example, a doctor judges that a child's fracture is due to abuse and predicts that x-rays may reveal signs of old fractures. This is not a highly probable prediction; many abused children reveal no such evidence. But this finding is highly unlikely in a child plucked at random from the population and with no known history of broken bones. Therefore finding evidence of old injuries is highly supportive of the hypothesis that the injury is non-accidental. Conversely, if the doctor predicts from the hypothesis that a young child is being abused that his mother will be in her twenties, then finding this is true offers little support because a high percentage of mothers of young children are in their twenties.

In the case of psychoanalysis, strong support is hard to find. The theories do not, on the whole, permit specific predictions. Inferring precise consequences is complicated by the conjectured role of 'defence mechanisms' such as projection and denial whereby aspects of the unconscious that are unacceptable to the conscious mind are converted into a tolerable form. Hence it can, for example, be predicted that an unresolved Oedipal conflict will manifest itself in overt behaviour but its specific form cannot be specified. Both a display of anger and one of affection towards one's father might be interpreted as evidence for the underlying conflict. Indeed the range of behaviour consistent with the hypothesis that someone has an unresolved Oedipal conflict is so great that, as Popper complained, whatever happens is consistent with it. Such evidence does not support the theory. The probability of any one item of behaviour is the same on background knowledge alone as it is given the psychoanalytic hypothesis.

Vague assessments and predictions by social workers run into similar trouble. The problem with a vague prediction is that any of a wide range of results can be consistent with it. Suppose a social worker helping a depressed client predicts that, with social work help, the client's social functioning will improve. Any sign of new behaviour might seem to the social worker evidence of improvement. But the probability of some change in behaviour is high whether or not the client receives social work help. On the other hand, if the social worker makes a precise prediction such as: 'the client will start taking her children to school', something which she has been unable to do for months, the prior probability of this happening without any help is significantly lower than its likelihood if the social worker is indeed helpful. Popper was correct in saying that theories that exclude no possible state of affairs cannot be falsified but neither can they receive inductive support.

Popper, like other philosophers, is concerned about the question of when scientists should abandon a theory. Popper's account of how scientists deal, or should deal, with refutations runs into difficulties because, when a prediction from a complex set of premises is found to be wrong, deductive logic alone does not offer any guide to which premise is at fault. This raises the possibility that the core theories can always be protected from refutation by rejecting or modifying lower level assumptions. Lakatos, with his talk of 'protective belts' makes it sound as if scientists are as dogmatically attached to their theories as Popper's analytic friends were to Freud. The Bayesian account, however, does provide an explanation of how scientists decide which premise to give up or modify. It shows how it can be rational, not dogmatic, to continue to retain a previously successful theory in the face of new falsifying evidence.

Howson and Urbach argue that when a set of premises have been falsified, it is possible to determine 'which hypothesis suffers most in the refutation' (1989, p. 97). Starting with the prior probabilities of the theory and the auxiliary hypotheses individually, it is possible, using probability calculus, to work out the posterior probability of each, given the falsifying evidence. Differences in the prior probabilities lead to sharply different effects on the posterior probabilities and scientists are justified in keeping the hypothesis with the highest probability.

The authors illustrate this with an example where the prior probability of the theory ($P(t)$), equals 0.9 – that is, scientists have considerable confidence in it – and the auxiliary hypothesis is deemed less probable, $P(a)$ equals 0.6. When new falsifying evidence is considered, the posterior probabilities are strikingly different. The theory becomes only slightly less likely – the probability drops to 0.8787. On the other hand, confidence in the auxiliary hypothesis is substantially reduced with a new probability of only 0.073. A substantial difference is found even when the prior probabilities are much closer. If the prior probability of the auxiliary hypothesis is kept at 0.6 and the theory's probability reduced to 0.7, the posterior probability of the theory drops a little to 0.65 while the auxiliary hypothesis slumps to 0.21. Given results like these, scientists decisions to keep the theory and modify the auxiliary hypothesis are reasonable.

Hence the behaviourist or psychoanalyst who has a single therapeutic failure and decides that it challenges assumptions made in the particular application rather than the core theory itself is not irrationally protecting a pet theory but acting reasonably given the assessment of the relative support for the theory and the assumptions.

JUDGING PROBABILITY IN SOCIAL WORK PRACTICE

Social workers can use the central concepts of the Bayesian approach to review their judgements more rigorously. They need not work out the mathematics formally – indeed, they would rarely be able to since, in most areas of social work, we lack the necessary detailed information. Even in the area of risk factors for child abuse, where statistics are available, local authority handbooks usually only list the risk factors without giving social workers specific information about their incidence. But, despite this, they can use the key ideas to help them estimate the weight of new evidence.

The inquiry into the death of Jasmine Beckford (London Borough of Brent, 1985) described the social workers as 'naive almost beyond belief' for failing to revise their optimistic judgement of Jasmine's parents and to see that Jasmine was suffering at home. This case provides an interesting illustration of how a Bayesian approach could be applied. Adopting a more stringent approach requires more than the individual social worker's commitment. Practitioners need work conditions in which management encourages and helps them to devote the necessary time and energy to critical review. It has been argued that the culture of social work organisations encourages practitioners to simplify their decision-making tasks by limiting the information they consider and promotes: 'selective ignorance, inattention, non-communication or incomprehension' (Dingwall, 1986, p. 492). The following discussion should not, therefore, be taken as a personal criticism of the workers involved in the Beckford case.

To begin with a summary of events: Jasmine, aged twenty months, and her sister Louise, aged three months, were taken into care in August 1981. Louise had been admitted to hospital with a broken arm and eye haemorrhages which were attributed to abuse. Three days later,

Jasmine was also admitted, with a broken leg. Her mother and stepfather said this was due to an accident and doctors were reluctant to rule this out. Place of Safety Orders were obtained and the children moved to a foster home while efforts were made to work with their parents. At this stage, there was considerable professional disagreement about the prospects for rehabilitation. Only the social workers showed much optimism. Full Care Orders were then made. At the hearing, an independent medical report said that X-rays had revealed an old fracture in Jasmine's arm strongly indicative of non-accidental injury. The magistrates making the order added a rider expressing the hope that the children would be re-united with their parents. Mr Beckford was convicted of assault on Louise and sentenced to six months imprisonment suspended for two years. The parents had supervised weekly access to their children. In March 1982 they were re-housed with the help of the social workers. In April, the case conference decided the children should return home on trial. To begin with, the social worker and a family aide visited daily. A place at a nursery was arranged for Jasmine. By May, a case review meeting was optimistically reducing the frequency of visits and setting revocation of the Care Orders as the long term objective. Mr Beckford was present and expressed resentment at the social work intrusion into their lives. The minutes of the meeting end with the judgement that there is no concern over the care of the children 'nor is it felt that they are at risk in their home on trial' (London Borough of Brent, 1985, p. 116). In November 1982, the case conference decided to remove the children's names from the 'at risk' register. Application was made to revoke the Care Orders in June 1983 but the Court refused on the grounds that it was too soon. The family aide was withdrawn in August 1983. The social worker continued to visit but the children were rarely present. Jasmine was seen fleetingly in September 1983 and again, briefly, in March 1984. On July 5th 1984, the social worker and her senior made strenuous, but unsuccessful, efforts to see the family to discuss revoking the Care Orders. That evening Jasmine was taken into hospital dead from head injuries. The postmortem revealed several fractures sustained at varying times during the preceding two years. Jasmine was also emaciated as a result of chronic undernourishment. Mr Beckford was convicted of manslaughter and Jasmine's mother, Miss Lorrington, of child neglect.

With hindsight, it is easy to see that Jasmine endured both physical abuse and poor care in her final two years but would the optimistic appraisal of the family have been maintained if the social workers had used a more critical approach? The answer is *no*. A more rigorous standard of reasoning, however, would have required pervasive and fundamental changes in the way they worked.

A basic weakness in the social work practice was the quality of the initial assessments of the family and the risk to the children. The inquiry complains that important information was ignored. The parents' educational history (in special schools) was not examined; psychiatric reports were not obtained; their failure to visit the children regularly in hospital as agreed was not questioned; nurses were not asked for their observations of the parent-child relationships. Besides only collecting a narrow range of information, the social workers did not make clear assessments. They appear to have decided fairly rapidly that the attack on Louise was a one-off episode but their reasons are obscure. Vague judgements are hard to test. They do not lead to any, even crude, predictions and so cannot receive strong support from new evidence. If, for instance, the assessment had been that the parents were generally adequate parents reacting to some extreme episode of stress then one could predict that further investigations of their parenting would support this. Social workers could note the frequency of their visits to the hospital and the nature of their interactions with their children, for example.

Another problem with vague assessments is that they cannot be falsified. Any new finding can be made consistent with them. In this case, the Beckfords had agreed to visit their children in hospital frequently but failed to do so. This raises questions about their parenting and their willingness to work with social workers. The social workers, however, did not appear to treat it as significant and ask why it was happening.

There were several stages at which there was strong evidence to challenge the optimistic social work assessments. The basic assumption that Louise had suffered a one-off attack was cast into some doubt by Jasmine's injury of uncertain causation three days later. It becomes even more unlikely when we add the medical information reported at the court hearing one month later that Jasmine's X-rays revealed old fractures that her parents had not divulged to anyone. This finding has a low incidence among abused children but a far lower one in non-abusive families so it should have increased the social workers' assessment of risk considerably. The new medical information seems, however, to have been ignored and the assessment unchanged.

The social work assessment was challenged at the time by other professionals but conflicting views led to hostility rather than constructive debate. Medical and nursing staff thought there was considerable risk of further abuse and were pessimistic about the likely success of rehabilitation. The professionals could have used the dispute as an opportunity to trying to understand each other's reasons for the differing assessments, a process that could have been very helpful in ensuring that a wider range of evidence was considered and its reliability questioned. With the Bayesian approach, these rival assessments of risk would have tended to converge as new evidence was received. The social workers' low probability of abuse would have risen sharply on learning of Jasmine's old injuries and so come closer to the medical assessment. However, in this case, the social workers' assessment was unchanged and the opposing view became silent. After the children had returned to their parents, only social work staff attended the conferences that decided on future actions, although these are usually multi-disciplinary.

Once the children were home, the social workers rapidly became confident about their safety. Was there evidence to support this? The inadequacy of the family assessment meant it was unclear what improvements, if any, social workers wanted to see or what circumstance they thought might indicate risk. From the information in the inquiry report, there was, however, considerable evidence to cause concern though it was not collected or recognised as significant by the social workers.

One factor highlighted by the inquiry was that, while at the foster home, Jasmine gained considerable weight having been seriously below average before. Since there was no medical explanation such as recovery from an illness for this weight increase, it raises questions about the adequacy of her previous care. Textbooks cite weight as a factor to measure in evaluating the success of being home on trial. If this had been done in Jasmine's case, her subsequent weight loss and poor development would have alerted social workers to her failure to thrive with her parents. Weight loss is not strongly predicted by the hypothesis that Jasmine was being abused (only a minority of abused children show it) but its probability in the absence of abuse or any known medical cause is extremely low so it increases the probability of abuse substantially. Since Jasmine was rarely seen by outsiders, her weight loss went unnoticed.

Another factor which appears relevant in this case is the parents' attitude to social workers and willingness to comply with social work plans to monitor the case. At the first conference after the children went home, Mr Beckford was showing hostility and complaining about the intrusion of social workers into their lives. Jasmine was supposed to attend a nursery but was frequently absent. In the final year of her life, she was only seen twice by the social worker, the mother offering various excuses for her absence. These issues were not followed up but accepted by the social workers.

This case illustrates a common feature in monitoring cases. Faulty assessments can be detected not just by some major incident such as new injuries but by seeing the accumulation of many small causes for concern. Each factor should reduce the probability of the optimistic assessment slightly and the cumulative effect is to cast serious doubt on it. In contrast, in this and several other child abuse cases, social workers dealt with each worrying incident in isolation and, having decided it did not falsify their judgement, they discounted it. They therefore failed to notice the growing signs for concern.

The case of Stephanie Fox (Wandsworth Area Child Protection Committee, 1990) also illustrates the tendency of social workers to discount evidence against their current beliefs once they have decided it is not major enough to make them change their minds. Stephanie returned home on trial having been in care because of abuse. She kept having bruises. Each, on its own, could be explained away as a typical accident to a young child. However, over the year she was at home, there were forty incidents of bruising. On four occasions, she had a black eye said to be due to running into a door. If the social workers had kept a record of all the slightly worrying incidents, they would have seen that the pattern was getting less and less like that of an unabused child having accidents.

Perhaps the most fundamental change that adopting a Bayesian approach requires is that social workers do not hold their beliefs as true or false but as more or less probable. They need to recognise their fallibility and to be open to criticism and revision of their judgements. In such a culture, rival views of a family are seen as non-threatening and possible sources of new important information. If one accepts that beliefs can be wrong, then there is clearly a need to test and monitor, with the expectation that evidence might tell against one's current view of the family. Small causes for concern may be considered insufficient to change the judgement but they affect the probability a little and can have a cumulative effect so that the judgement is finally overthrown.

CONCLUSION

Scientific theories cannot be proved conclusively true but can become more probable as evidence supports them. By the same token, social workers can never be certain that their understanding of clients is accurate but can increase their confidence by looking for evidence for and against their theories.

It is psychologically unsettling to recognise that the foundations of one's social work practice are fallible. Theories may be only more or less probable but social workers have to use them as the basis for decisive action. A child may be only probably at risk but social workers have to decide whether or not to remove him from his parents. It may be temptingly comforting to believe that one is 'right' when making such harsh decisions but over-confidence is dangerous. Social workers can be right in the sense that they have made the best decision on the available evidence but, as the turkey found when Christmas approached, the best judgement can be wrong.

The fallibility of social work theories and judgements has important implications. Fallible judgements need to be tested, reviewed, and changed in the light of new evidence. They can only be tested if they are clearly articulated so that some predictions can be deduced. Counter evidence may not be strong enough to overthrow a judgement but it casts some doubt and should be recorded and included in future appraisals.

CHAPTER 8

The Importance of the Social Context

Raynor accuses empiricists of having 'one eye closed' (1984, p. 1) because, he argues, while empirical research 'may help to improve the technical efficacy of methods, it can tell us little about the desirability of the goals towards which our methods are directed, or the social functions they serve'. Empirical research is, indeed, only part of the total picture. Raynor's criticism rests on a misunderstanding of the claims made by empiricists. None would hold that empiricist methods, on their own, can settle all the complex decisions social workers face about who to help and what methods to use. Science will not produce a neutral body of knowledge that will wholly determine who deserves help and which methods are the best to use. These issues also involve moral, political and economic factors.

This chapter begins by considering the numerous factors that influence social work decisions. All would agree that the social context of social work has a major impact on what social workers do. But one group of people, the relativists, claim that the social context is all-important and deny even a limited role for empirical knowledge. Many of these writers describe their view as 'postmodern'.

This term, however, has a broad and varied range of meanings. One universal element is a rejection of a positivist account of science. Some then coninue to endorse science though in a revised empirical form (e.g. Rorty, 1991, p. 202). In this sense, I could be described as a postmodernist. But the majority of postmodernists, especially in the social work literature, take a relativist view of knowledge (Howe, 1994; Pardeck, Murphy and Choi, 1994; Parton, 1994; Pozatek, 1994). They maintain that the philosophical arguments against the positivist view of science also undermine the whole scientific claim to being empirical and, hence, to producing knowledge that is, in any way, more reliable than other forms of wisdom. I shall refer to these writers as relativists rather than postmodernists to avoid any ambiguity and because it is that aspect of their view that is of interest in this chapter.

Relativism has been used to argue for radical changes in social work. Social workers are urged to treat the case for a scientific approach with scepticism and to adopt whatever style of reasoning they prefer. All forms of knowledge, relativists claim, can be judged only according to their internal criteria of justification; there are no universal criteria of rationality by which rival forms of thought can be compared. Hence science cannot be judged better than intuition. In social work, relativists claim, decisions are not just partly influenced by value judgements, as empiricists would say, but are determined by them.

Social work relativists give us little detail of the philosophical background to their claims. A survey of the literature shows that Kuhn is by far the most frequently cited philosopher (though usually only in a footnote). Feyerabend (who takes a similar but slightly more radical position than Kuhn) comes a distant second, while Paley (1987) briefly mentions Wittgenstein. Therefore, in rebutting the relativists' arguments, I shall concentrate on their interpretation of Kuhn's philosophy of science.

Relativists' attack on the rationality of science has two strands: first, as mentioned in Chapter Six, the argument that there is no independent empirical evidence by which to test a theory and, secondly, a claim that there are no universal, rational criteria by which the evidence can be weighed. Deciding whether or not to accept a theory, relativists claim, is not a rational process but determined by social and psychological factors. Howe alleges that 'dominant forms of understanding are based on social processes rather than empirical validity' (1987).

There is clearly an inherent contradiction in using relativism as the basis for criticising one particular form of reasoning (science). If there are no universal criteria for comparing different cultures, or language games, or whatever category knowledge is said to be relative to, then relativists cannot judge science by any independent criteria. Relativism as a doctrine must itself be only relative to a particular viewpoint. Yet Howe and Paley use relativism to justify their campaign for attacking empiricism and championing rival forms of reasoning in social work. The coherence of their arguments for such radical changes in social work will be considered before examining the strength of the philosophical foundations of relativism.

THE INFLUENCE OF VALUES

For empiricists in social work, decisions about what to do involve consideration of both empirical issues and value judgements. Social workers need to evaluate explanatory theories and therapeutic approaches and decide which ones are most probable or effective. They also have to decide on the aims of their interventions, who to help and how. In this area, empirical studies are only one of many relevant factors.

The social context is clearly of vital importance in social work since society decides 'who social workers are allowed to deal with' (Philp, 1979, p. 98). Legislation defines the duties and powers of the profession. It dictates which people are seen as in need of care, and which are deviant and in need of control. Politicians decide what financial resources should be put into the personal social services and which client groups should be treated as a priority at any time. Senior managers make further decisions about resource allocation and priority groups. Individual social workers also contribute to the chain of decision-making that culminates in particular clients receiving particular services. Political views, economic factors and moral values all play a part in determining the final outcomes. Empirical knowledge provides only one element, though a very important one, in the overall debates within social work about the focus of work.

The definition of social problems is, in large part, a social process. At a particular time, certain types of social problems or individual troubles arouse concern. The nature of that concern may variously lead to the desire to control, or cure, or care for those experiencing the problems. Explanatory theories of how the problem behaviour has been produced play a part in shaping society's view of the problem. As Gambrill (1990) comments, the same type of behaviour has, at different times, been called sinful, then criminal, then an indication of mental illness. Explanatory theories effect what response is considered appropriate.

Firm evidence that a particular method of resolving a social problem is effective does not, on its own, determine that that method should be used. Debates about rival theories in the natural sciences typically involve theories that are rivals in the sense that they are inconsistent, that is, they cannot both be true. Rival theories of this sort occur in the social sciences, a classic conflict being between psychoanalytic and behavioural theories. However, many theories are complementary rather than conflicting. Human behaviour is generally thought to have a complex causation and different theories often focus on different strands of causation. For example, a theory which connects juvenile delinquency to family dynamics usually claims only to identify an important causal factor rather than offering a total explanation. It is compatible with theories explaining delinquency in terms of other factors, such as biological processes or peer group pressures. The various theories suggest different ways of helping: by focusing on the family, for instance, or physical health or the peer group. Evidence of effectiveness is only one, albeit important, consideration when deciding which aspect to try to change.

There has been a classic debate in social work about where to direct efforts to alter the situation. Should it be the individual, society, or some combination who changes? Stevenson points out: 'surely it is obvious that individual, familial, social and material factors play a part, albeit in differing proportions, in the problems which social workers experience?' (1989, p. 159). Over the decades, opinions about the appropriate targets for change have shifted. In the late 1960s, for example, the radical movement in social work argued that the dominant focus on the family and individual in social work practice served to maintain an unequal society (Corrigan and Leonard, 1978).

The value-free claims of science are also limited. Theory development is influenced by scientists' presuppositions and interests. Scientists do not approach the world with an empty mind and build up theories on the basis of neutral observation. They already have some assumptions about the subject area they want to study.

The influence of pre-existing beliefs or values can be even greater when studying social issues than in the

natural sciences. Theoretical explanations will often refer
to issues on which people already have some opinions. A
theory linking crime to unemployment levels would
endorse existing views for some while challenging deeply
held convictions for others. Theories in the natural sciences can sometimes support or conflict with people's
interests or moral views – the link between cancer and
cigarette smoking, for instance – but, as Papineau points
out, social science theories almost invariably have some
relevance for existing views:

> By the nature of their subject matter the claims made
> by theories in the social sciences cannot help but be
> about the empirical connections between various
> states of affairs that different groups will be
> interested in preserving or preventing. (1978, p. 176)

Science's claim to being value free rests not on the way
that theories are developed but on how they are tested.
Strong political or moral views may influence the formation of a theory about the causes of crime. They may also
make it easier for researchers to get funding to publicise
and test the theory. But the theory will not stand up to
empirical testing just because politicians, or other
interested parties, want it to. The 'short, sharp shock'
punishment was confidently expected by Conservative
ministers to reduce recidivism but, however powerful
their convictions, empirical studies have not produced the
desired result.

RELATIVISTS IN SOCIAL WORK

Paley (1987) presents an ardent attack on the scientific
movement in social work, detailing the philosophical
background to his views. He bases his rejection of empiricism on relativist interpretations of Kuhn's philosophy
of science and Wittgenstein's private language argument.

His argument has two strands: the claim that there is no common language between rival theorists and hence no shared facts against which theories can be judged, and, secondly, the contention that there are no shared criteria of rationality to use in judging rival theories.

Paley urges the non-scientific majority in social work to see the value assigned to scientific knowledge as based on cultural rather than epistemological factors. He restates the art/science debate in terms of a power struggle between the academic world and the world of practice, inciting practitioners to defend their position. Academics who criticise practice, he says, are using scientific criteria but social workers do not, on the whole, share their scientific beliefs and therefore need not take their criticisms seriously. I imagine that, to Paley, an academic's advice to social workers to look for independent empirical evidence of their intuitive judgements is like a Moslem encouraging a Christian to attend the mosque.

Paley's relativism has far-reaching implications for social work. He rules out any hope of developing a body of knowledge or of being able to 'identify anything that could be "taught to future generations of social workers"' (1987, p. 182). He suggests that the only useful research is sociological not evaluative, finding out what social workers do and how they evaluate their work. Their evaluative methods should not themselves be judged, however, by any outside criteria such as scientific ones.

Howe (1987) also illustrates the extensive repercussions of adopting relativism in social work. He has written an introductory text on social work theories for students which, taking a relativist line, relegates scientific methods to being one approach among many equally valid ones. Therefore, in presenting theories to students, Howe does not consider any questions about their truth or probability. The decision about which theories to adopt is left to the individual student who 'pays her money and takes her choice' (1987, p. 166). Her decision though, Howe thinks, will by influenced by her social context: 'theories', he claims, 'emerge as products of their time and place' (1987, p. 167).

The aim of Howe's book is to help students make an informed choice between theories by clarifying the political nature of the type of practice they lead to and offering some guidance on their psychological appeal. The 'fixers', for instance, aim at maintaining current social systems while the 'revolutionaries' want to reform them.

However, this way of classifying theories begs the question of whether the different theories have their intended effects. Our values may lead us to prefer one theory to another and to *hope* that it is true or that a particular therapeutic approach will work, but the world does not necessarily conform to our wishes. The 'fixers' will only achieve their aim of maintaining social stability *if their methods work.*

Howe touches on the issues of truth and probability in an inconsistent way. In spite of presenting a concern for empirical evidence and for testing theories as just features of some [scientific] theories in social work, he does think they have a particular merit: they lead to more effective ways of helping people. In describing changes in medical theories, he asserts that later theories are better because they 'allow more efficacious treatments (1987, p. 11). Similarly, in discussing behavioural social work, he says:

If social workers want to be effective they have to find effective cures. The rigorous and exacting methods of science will help social workers identify treatment procedures that lead to behavioural cures. (1987, p. 59)

But who does not want to be effective? No social worker is interested merely in studying people but wants to help them. The Marxist, feminist or Rogerian social worker all want to act and to have some impact on the problems they have identified. Howe's views are puzzling. If scientific methods do indeed help social workers identify effective ways of helping, should they not be widely adopted? Perhaps he mistakenly thinks of science as a narrow, positivist discipline that cannot be used by Marxists or feminists, or others concerned with studying the subjective world of mental experience. Otherwise, as a relativist, his praise of science seems out of place.

Before examining the philosophical foundations of relativism, let us consider the coherence of its use in social work. The relativist thesis has generally been used in social work to attack science, to undermine its claims to producing reliable theories and to oppose the empiricist movement. But how can a relativist justify criticising a particular form of reasoning? The main claim of relativism is that cultures, disciplines or language games can only be judged by *internal* criteria; there are said to be no neutral, universal criteria. When Paley speaks disparagingly of empiricists as 'imperialists', by what standards is he judging them? If scientists claim to produce reliable knowledge, how can this claim be questioned except by people within the scientific culture?

The philosopher Hilary Putnam has called attention to the fundamental incoherence of relativists' arguments. They are attempting to say that 'from a God's-Eye View, there is no God's-Eye View' (1992, p. 25), to assert as a universal principle that there are no universal principles. They do not treat their own relativist views as themselves relative to their particular group: 'they know very well that the majority of their cultural peers are not convinced by Relativist arguments, but they keep on arguing because they think they are *justified* in doing so' (1992, p. 22) and they do not link the notion of justification to the majority opinion of the cultural group. If they did, they would accept their own views as mistaken.

Social work advocates of relativism, like relativists in general, seem aware that they are proposing a new account of rationality that challenges the existing views but believe, nevertheless, that it is in some way *better* than the currently dominant view. Paley (1987) and Howe (1987 and 1994) go to great lengths to present justifications for their views; they want to convince the reader that their account is superior to non-relativist views. But if scientists believe that they *do* produce more reliable theories than other disciplines, how can relativists claim they are misguided. How can a relativist talk of any rationality being *better* than another?

This is not just a quibble but a major issue for relativists. Howe (1994, p. 524) argues against the existence of 'underlying principles that can be used to judge the legitimacy of each competing world view' but then questions the legitimacy of the claims of scientists to acquiring objective knowledge. He tells social workers that no group should 'attempt to define the experience of another group' but then says that all groups who believe that they have access to 'the truth' are wrong: 'there are no centres of authority and truth'. To imply that religious believers, for example, are mistaken in their fundamental beliefs is to break his own rule and to define their experience in a radically different way from their own view.

The tolerance of different values and beliefs encouraged by relativists also has significant implications for social workers. At first glance, it has a pleasing liberalism, encouraging people to treat other cultures with respect, but it also denies that there are any rational grounds for challenging other people's beliefs and moral views. Yet this is a common feature of social work. Far from accepting the majority view of the particular culture to which they belong, social workers are often in the position of opposing it and defending minority groups and minority views. Their clients are among the most disadvantaged and discriminated against in society. Most social workers, for instance, find racism abhorrent; they think it is morally wrong to regard some people as inferior and to treat them unequally because of their ethnic group. And yet they recognise that racist views are widely held in our society. Most would argue that their opposition to racism is 'right', not just in some limited sense that it is a moral belief in their own peer group that happens to conflict with the majority but in an absolute sense. Many would also argue that white people hold many false beliefs about black people: that black men are more violent than white men, for instance. They would want to challenge these false beliefs, citing empirical evidence against them, and consider they have convincing, rational grounds for saying they are inaccurate.

Relativism as a doctrine seems to lead to paralysis, to an inability to judge human efforts at making sense of the world and to a denial of any possibility of making progress. Let us now look at the underlying arguments for such a far-reaching doctrine.

KUHN'S PHILOSOPHY OF SCIENCE
The three key features of Kuhn's philosophy are the concept of paradigms, normal and revolutionary periods in science, and the notion that two paradigms are incommensurable.

Kuhn conceives of scientists working within a complex structure which he calls a paradigm. Scientists who share a paradigm are working on the same theoretical system but share far more than this: they agree on what procedures and techniques to use in applying a theory; they share metaphysical principles, values and attitudes. Paradigms 'are the sources of the methods, problem-field, and standards of solutions accepted by any mature scientific community at any given time' (Kuhn, 1970, p. 103).

Kuhn makes an important distinction between two periods in science: normal and revolutionary times. Most of the time, scientists in a particular subject area work within a common paradigm. Unlike Popper's picture of scientists striving continually to falsify their theories, Kuhn argues that, in a period of normal science, the paradigm is generally accepted without question and counter-evidence is always interpreted as refuting some auxiliary hypothesis. The Bayesian account says that the basic theories *are* tested by the experiments but, because of their greater probability, scientists rationally decide that falsifications challenge lower level hypotheses. Kuhn describes the situation more as a gentlemen's agreement to assume the truth of the core ideas. Scientists, he says, are not trying to test the paradigm but to extend and improve its explanatory power. When they apply it in a new domain, they are involved in what he calls puzzle-solving, using the term to indicate that they assume the truth of the paradigm and try to make it fit the data. Any falsifications will be seen as indicating a fault in the auxiliary theories. The scientist's aim is to think of adaptations in these lower level theories which will make the paradigm and the evidence consistent. The challenge in normal science is to the ingenuity of the scientist rather than the truth of the core assumptions of the paradigm:

> If it [the paradigm] fails the test, only his own ability not the corpus of current science is impugned. In short, though tests occur frequently in normal science, these tests are of a peculiar sort, for in the final analysis it is the individual scientist rather than the current theory which is tested. (Kuhn, 1970, p. 5)

If scientists cannot devise a way of altering lower level assumptions in the light of the falsification, they will not necessarily look critically at the central assumptions of the paradigm. History shows that they will often leave the awkward result on one side as an anomaly and concentrate on areas in which the paradigm continues to be fruitful.

At times of revolution, however, the paradigm is reappraised. Confidence in it is weakened, perhaps by an accumulation of anomalies. People start to question its accuracy or ability to deal with the phenomena; they look around for alternative ideas; possibly then a rival paradigm is created. Some scientists will opt for the new paradigm and then a revolution will take place. At the end of it, one of the paradigms will have gained ascendancy as Einsteinian physics did over Newtonian. Scientific revolutions are when 'an older paradigm is replaced in whole or in part by an incompatible new one' (Kuhn, 1970, p. 92). A new period of normal science then begins within the victorious paradigm.

Kuhn was concerned mainly with the natural sciences and there are significant differences in the social sciences. Behaviourism and psychoanalytic theories can be seen as different paradigms in psychology but, unlike in the natural sciences, neither has clearly gained supremacy. They are still rivals after many decades; no period of 'normal' science has occurred when all working in the subject area agree on the paradigm in which to work.

Revolutionary changes from one paradigm to another are the distinguishing feature of Kuhn's philosophy and the point at which relativism appears to enter his philosophy in his earlier writings. He introduces the concept of 'incommensurability' to describe the radical differences between paradigms. The standard empirical account of judging rival theories or, in Kuhn's terms, paradigms considers that they can be compared in relation to their explanatory power, their ability to make accurate predictions. Kuhn, however, claims that scientists working in different paradigms are unable to compare their paradigms in this way because they are incommensurable. He argues that they are incommensurable in that the meaning of all terms change with paradigm change so there is no common body of empirical evidence against which the paradigms can be judged. They are also incommensurable, he claims, in that standards as well as meanings vary between paradigms: there are no independent criteria of what counts as a good explanation and hence comparisons cannot be made. Accepting a paradigm involves judging that it is better than its rival but, although matters of evidence and logic will influence this judgement, it is ultimately due to the psychology of the individual and the dynamics of the scientific group to which he belongs:

> As in political revolution, so in paradigm choice – there is no standard higher than the assent of the relevant community. To discover how scientific revolutions are effected, we shall therefore have to examine not only the impact of nature and of logic, but also the techniques of persuasive argumentation effective within the quite special groups that constitute the community of scientists. (Kuhn, 1970, p. 94)

The incommensurablity thesis appeared to most readers to imply a relativist view of science though Kuhn himself has always argued against this. The claims that meanings and standards vary between paradigms have been severely criticised and Kuhn himself, through a combination of clarifying and altering his position, has placed his philosophy within the empirical movement.

INCOMMENSURABLE LANGUAGE

Kuhn describes a paradigm as a shared world view. In his earlier writing, Kuhn meant this more or less literally:

> In a sense that I am unable to explicate further, the proponents of competing paradigms practice their trades in different worlds ... practising in different worlds, the two groups of scientists see different things when they look from the same point in the same direction. (Kuhn, 1970, p. 150)

This point of view follows from his theory of meaning. As discussed in Chapter Six, it is widely accepted that all observational terms involve some assumptions and do not get their meaning just from corresponding with the world. Relativists, like empiricists, reject the positivists' correspondence theory of meaning for observation terms. Unlike empiricists, however, they extend the holistic theory of meaning to *all* terms. Although relativists are among the most vociferous critics of positivism, 'the irony is', Newton-Smith points out, 'that Kuhn and Feyerabend have inherited from positivism the general holistic conception of the meaning of a term as given by the role of the term within a theory' (1981, p. 155).

The relativists' view of scientific advance is not of theory being tested against the hard data of reality and being corroborated or falsified. So-called empirical tests do not expose a theory to external adjudication but check one part of the theory against another. The terms which are classed as observational are part of an all-embracing structure in which the meaning of every term is connected with the others. Which terms are regarded as observational is more a question of the confidence scientists have in a particular aspect of the whole at a particular time; it is not due to their relationship with the world. Richard Rorty, defending this view, stresses:

The holistic point that words take their meanings from other words rather than by virtue of their representative character, and the corollary that vocabularies acquire their privileges from the men who use them rather than from their transparency to the real. (1979, p. 368)

Judging rival paradigms becomes problematic because, it is claimed, there is no shared level of evidence by which to weigh their relative success. If there is a change of paradigm, then, because words get their meaning from their position within the paradigm, *all* words change their meaning. Taking Newtonian and Einsteinian physics as an example, as Newton-Smith critically comments:

Not only do they mean something different by 'mass'; they also mean something different by 'the needle points at 4', 'look it's turned green', and so on. (Newton-Smith, 1981, p. 12)

If we apply this idea to theories familiar to social workers, taking psychoanalytic theory and learning theory as rival paradigms, it does not just imply the expected result that analysts and behaviourists will differ about what they mean by reports which are clearly theoretical such as 'this person has repressed his anger' or 'this behaviour is positively reinforced by the actor's environment'; it implies that they will mean something different when apparently using the same words, such as saying that 'this is a person X and 'this person says he is worried'. With this holistic theory of meaning, then, there is no common language between people in different paradigms in which we can state the evidence and so comparisons cannot be made.

For many critics of this holistic theory of meaning, Newton-Smith reports, 'its consequences are sufficiently absurd to justify its rejection' (1981, p. 157). More specific objections are made as well.

Kuhn tried to avoid some of these absurdities by claiming that the meanings of terms only change when we have a paradigm shift but that it stays constant through the 'minor' modifications scientists make as they work within a paradigm. If small alterations led to meaning change then it would be difficult for any scientist to find a colleague who spoke the same language but it seems clear that they do communicate. Although some such concession looks essential, Kuhn is criticised for his response:

> Kuhn does not provide an adequate criterion for determining how much change is required before there is a change in paradigm. This means that he has not provided a means of determining which theory changes generate variation in meaning. (Newton-Smith, 1981, p. 155)

This leads to difficulties for his theory of meaning. Psychoanalysis and behavioural psychology are generally accounted different paradigms. But the question arises whether, within psychoanalysis, the shift from Freud to Adler is a minor one or sufficient to warrant claiming that they meant different things by their common terms. Or should even the changes Freud himself made in his theories be judged enough to imply that the older Freud saw the world differently from the younger Freud? Kuhn offers no guidance on this point.

Kuhn's views are also criticised for conflicting so sharply with scientific practice. Scientists working on different theories show every sign of being able to communicate and to agree on a level of observation reports.

Putnam (1981, p. 114) objects to the Kuhnian incommensurability thesis because, he argues, it rules out translation of any kind: between paradigms, between cultures, and even between older forms of our own language and the present day. However, it is possible to translate and we can understand others, Putnam claims, pointing out that even Kuhn assumes he can talk meaningfully and in a paradigm-neutral way when he presents his incommensurability thesis. Kuhn cites Galileo as an example of someone with a different paradigm from our own and therefore, if his thesis is true, with no language in common with us. However Kuhn then finds no difficulty in talking about Galileo's ideas, believing both that he is giving an accurate account and that we shall have no difficulty in understanding him. Putnam complains: 'to tell us that Galileo had "incommensurable" notions and *then to go on to describe them at length* is totally incoherent' (1981, p. 115).

Putnam offers an empiricist critique of this concept of incommensurable language. He suggests that proponents of the holistic theory of meaning are confusing or conflating 'concept' and 'conception'. The concept or the reference of a term stays constant through translation although the conception, our associated beliefs about it may change:

> When we translate a word as, say temperature we equate the reference ... with that of our own term 'temperature' at least as we use it in that context. ...
> But so doing is compatible with the fact that the seventeenth-century scientists, or whoever, may have had a different conception of temperature, that is a different set of beliefs about it and its nature than we do. (Putnam, 1981, p. 117)

In his later writing, Kuhn has moved towards this empiricist account, accepting that terms do not completely change their reference when one paradigm supersedes another although associated beliefs may alter. Paradigms can, therefore, be compared: 'comparing theories ... demands only the identification of reference' (Kuhn, 1976, p. 191).

INCOMMENSURABLE STANDARDS

In his earlier writing, Kuhn seemed to claim that paradigms are also incommensurable in that standards, as well as meanings, vary between paradigms. This is how most of his readers interpreted his account. Lakatos provides a typical reading of what Kuhn appears to be saying about choosing between rival paradigms:

> Each paradigm contains its own standards. The crisis sweeps away not only the old theories and rules but also the standards which made us respect them. The new paradigm brings a totally new rationality. The change is a bandwagon effect. Thus, *in Kuhn's view scientific revolution is irrational, a matter of mob psychology.* (in Lakatos and Musgrave, 1970, p. 178)

Applying this interpretation to rival methods in social work, Kuhn seems to be claiming that choosing between, say, behaviour modification techniques and client-centred therapy cannot be based on a rational assessment of their relative effectiveness. Behaviourists may point out that their approach is better supported by empirical evidence but relativists, such as Howe, can maintain that they are judging it by a criterion that is internal to their behavioural paradigm.

Kuhn has strongly objected to this understanding of his work. He denies saying that theory-choice is irrational: 'reports of this sort manifest total misunderstanding' (1978, Chapter 13). His subsequent comments are intended as a clarification, not a revision, of his views, though many commentators have claimed that they, in fact, mark a major change in his position. The point he was trying to make, he says, is that, although there are scientific criteria for theory-choice, they do not determine a specific answer which all rational scientists must accept. It is possible to reject a new paradigm without being irrational or unscientific. He cites his argument in his first book:

> Lifelong resistance (to a new theory) ... is not a violation of scientific standards. Though the historian can always find men, Priestley, for instance, who were unreasonable to resist as long as they did, he will not find a point at which resistance becomes illogical or unscientific. (1970, p. 320)

He does not, he claims, think that all standards vary between paradigms. On the contrary, his study of the history of science has shown there is considerable consistency in how scientists in different ages and paradigms judge theories. He lists five such criteria 'not because they are exhaustive, but because they are individually important and collectively sufficiently varied to indicate what is at stake':

> First, a theory should be accurate: within its domain, that is, consequences deducible from a theory should be in demonstrated agreement with the results of existing experiments and observations. Second, a theory should be consistent, not only internally or with itself, but also with other currently accepted theories .... Third, it should have broad scope: in particular, a theory's consequences should extend far beyond the particular observations, laws, or subtheories it was initially designed to explain. Fourth, and closely related, it should be simple, bringing order to phenomena that, in its absence, would be individually isolated .... Fifth, a theory should be fruitful of new research findings. (1978, p. 321)

In the social sciences, where no single paradigm has become supreme, the rivals can be compared but the rational criteria do not lead to a determinate answer about which one should be selected.

The practical implications of Kuhn's account of scientific practice (that is, of what scientists should actually do if his account is correct) is similar to the Bayesian one but he offers a very different rationale for it. Kuhn thinks that the criteria are values that are 'in part learned from experience and they evolve with it' (1978, p. 335) and that are influential because of their general acceptance. The Bayesian account, however, provides a rationale for why these values and not others have become accepted by linking them to the probability calculus.

As Kuhn has developed and modified his philosophy in the past two decades, he has clearly moved away from the relativist interpretation of his early work. He now, like other empiricists, holds the view that there is a transcultural, or, in his terms, a 'nonparadigmatic', notion of how to appraise theories. Putnam summarises the shift in his views:

> We no longer find Kuhn speaking of Gestalt switches . . . . The idea that paradigm shifts are just things that happen has been replaced by the idea that it can be *justified* to start looking for a paradigm to replace one's existing paradigm, and it can be justified to decide that one has found a good paradigm to serve as a replacement. (1992, p. 125)

CONCLUSION

The bulk of this chapter has been concerned with examining the relativists' attack on science and on its contribution to social work. Relativists deny the existence of any universal standards of rationality and argue that all forms of knowledge can be judged only by internal criteria. Social work relativists then go on to attack the claims of empiricists about the reliability of scientific knowledge and to encourage social workers to oppose their 'imperialist' activities. It is unclear what criteria they are using for criticising science though the impression gained from their writings is that they believe they are making some universal (non-relativist) points about the limits of human reasoning. They are, in Putnam's terms, trying to say 'from a God's-Eye View there is no God's-Eye View'.

The philosophical basis for their relativism is shaky. Most social work relativists cite Kuhn's philosophy of science as justification but his early work has been severely criticised and Kuhn himself, through a mixture of clarifying and altering his initial views, now clearly supports a non-relativist view of science.

Empirical knowledge has only a limited role within the whole process of making decisions in social work about who should receive help and what methods should be used. The relative effectiveness of different helping strategies is a significant factor but interventions also need to be judged in terms of political, moral and economic factors. Values pervade social work and moral debates are an essential and permanent feature of practice. The empirical social work movement does not claim to provide a neutral body of knowledge that will determine what social workers should do, bypassing any need to confront the complex ethical dilemmas of practice. Those debates, however, will be made easier if workers are clearer about what they are doing and their reasoning. A more public style of working will not only aid empirical research but also enrich public discussion of the goals and methods of social work.

CHAPTER 9
Empirical Reflective Practice

Debates about social work expertise are important because the profession has become so important in the lives of people in trouble. Those with disabilities and physical or mental illness, children suffering abuse and neglect, parents having difficulty in coping, all are directed to social work and hope to receive practical or psychological help with their problems. Providing effective help is the ambition of all social workers but human problems are hard to solve. Resource constraints are an obvious limit on what social workers can achieve. Some clients live in appalling social conditions that are beyond the scope of a social worker to alter. But social workers are also limited by their understanding of human conduct and their knowledge of how to help people change.

There have always been discussions in the profession about the nature of social work knowledge and expertise. Visions of social work's purpose have varied as have views about how to be scientific. For many years, the art/science debate was sharply polarised. On one side, a small band, mainly academics, were advocating a positivist/behavioural model of scientific social work that was radically at odds with what most social workers were doing. On the other side, the majority of social workers were continuing to rely mainly on their empathic and intuitive skills in direct work with clients and could see no way that these skills could be reconciled with the behaviourist approach. The debate today is fundamentally different; the empirical movement, based on current ideas in the philosophy of science, differs substantially from the positivist one. Social workers are not being encouraged to reject their current ways of working but to develop them by using scientific standards of reasoning. They are not being told to throw away their practice wisdom but to evaluate it more rigorously. Empathy is not despised as unscientific but valued as a rich, though highly fallible, source of ideas. Intuitive reasoning is seen as essential but its accuracy can be increased by careful analysis and review of its underlying assumptions.

In the past, scientific social work was strongly associated with empirical research. In the 1960s and 1970s, large-scale trials of social work interventions were the most prominent evidence of efforts to put social work on a scientific footing. These involved outside researchers studying practice and producing results that practitioners were then expected to act upon. Such studies will always have a place, especially in relation to judging whether client improvement was due to natural history or the social work service. But nowadays, the main focus of the knowledge debate is on direct practice with clients. Social workers are not being urged to allow researchers to evaluate their practice by scientific standards but to use those standards themselves.

One reason is that earlier research had severely limited practical value because it was of the 'black box' variety: the type of social work help being evaluated was insufficiently detailed. All that could be concluded in many cases was that whatever had gone on in the black box labelled 'social work help' had had a particular effect.

Consequently, the greater priority at present is seen to be 'the important task of clearly identifying the nature of the input' (Sheldon, 1982, p. 8). Only when social workers have been able to describe their ways of working clearly can large-scale studies produce the kind of detailed findings that will have clear practical implications.

Another reason for the focus on direct practice is that scientific methods are not just useful in evaluating outcomes but in improving the quality of practice at all stages. By moving from a private, intuitive style to a more explicit, critical approach, social workers can increase the accuracy of their assessments, decisions, and reviews.

In order to use scientific standards of reasoning, social workers need, first, to make their practice wisdom explicit, to put their reasoning into words. Greater clarity will make it easier to test and evaluate their reasoning but it will help in many other ways as well. It will permit practice wisdom to be shared more within the profession. At present, many insights are held by the experienced practitioner and conveyed to others, if at all, only through direct contact, in supervision perhaps or in case discussions with colleagues.

Clients will also benefit from more clarity. They are increasingly being considered as partners in arranging social care. If they can better understand how social workers are viewing them and how they reach their decision, they will be able to influence the process more.

Being more explicit will help social workers defend themselves from what is often felt to be the intrusion of management. In order to monitor social workers closely, managers are devising information systems that, at present, many social workers feel are distorting or undervaluing the aspects of practice which they themselves consider the most valuable. By being clearer about what they are doing and the reasons for it, they can ensure monitoring includes the information they consider central to good practice.

Greater public understanding of what social workers do will also influence society's expectations of social work. Social work takes place in a social context where moral, political and economic arguments affect what social workers are asked to do. These debates would benefit from a better contribution from social workers about what they believe they can do, of their strengths and limits.

Resistance to making practice wisdom explicit comes partly from a misconception of science. With strict behaviourism as a model, many social workers mistakenly believe that science deals only with observable entities. Their theorising about what is going on in people's minds therefore does not seem compatible with a scientific approach. Science can and does have theories that refer to objects or processes that are not directly observable. But developing explicit theories from practice wisdom, although possible, is not easy. Science offers no mechanical way of generating hypotheses and theories. Asking practitioners to formulate their methods is not simply asking for a description of what they do. It is asking them to say which of the many things they do they think are causally significant in helping clients. There may be disagreement. Freudians, for instance, would consider that the content of their interpretations was the key factor whereas Rogerians would dispute this, arguing that it is not what they say but the relationship within which they say it that produces change. It takes intellectual effort, imagination and creativity to speculate about what factors of practice have an impact on clients.

Nor is it possible to form clear theories from imprecise thinking. The evidence from research suggests that much practice rests on incomplete assessments and hazy plans. For some social workers therefore being more explicit will not just involve making their reasoning public but adopting a more reflective, purposeful style of working.

The language in which social workers express their reasoning is crucial both in relation to testing their ideas and to communicating them. For many years, the loudest message from those in favour of science has been that they should reduce all their concepts to behavioural terms. But since the positivists' theory of meaning has been severely criticised and rejected, the old behavioural principle is also rejected. However, the positivists' strategies of reducing complex concepts and operationally defining them, while flawed, are useful as ways of clarifying concepts. It must also be remembered that, in science, concept formation and theory development go hand in hand. Social workers should not see themselves as having to face the daunting task of trying to start by expressing their ideas in precise terms but can aim to make them progressively clearer as they use and refine their hypotheses. For instance, the concept of high expressed emotion can now be measured with high inter-rater agreement but began in a much vaguer form, being made more precise as research was carried out on families with a member with schizophrenia and theories about its importance in relapse were developed.

In testing hypotheses and theories, the key factors are the range, reliability and validity of the evidence. Reasoning intuitively, social workers are likely to make the common human error of noticing evidence that supports their beliefs. Facts that challenge them tend to be either overlooked or, if seen, discredited in some way so that they can be ignored. In contrast, scientists try to falsify their theories. They work out the empirical implications and then, by experiment or observation, check whether the world is, indeed, as predicted by their theory. In a similar way, social workers can assess a client or family and then consider what other facts they would expect to find if that assessment is correct.

The positivists' claim that only behavioural measures were scientifically acceptable posed a harsh demand that most social workers, with good reason, considered they could not meet. The current emphasis on looking for reliable, valid evidence presents a more feasible task. Social workers in busy daily practice may well be unable to collect evidence to the same standard as a researcher but they can still strive to check their findings more carefully, to search for counter evidence more vigorously, and so make their evidence more reliable.

Weighing the evidence in science and in social work is complex. Scientific theories cannot be proven with certainty. Finding supportive evidence and failing to find falsifications, despite searching for them, provide grounds for having more confidence in a theory. There are, however, disputes in philosophy about how to judge the degree of confidence offered by the evidence and when to reject a theory. The Bayesian approach, presented in this book, argues that scientists reason in accordance with the probability calculus. This approach provides a clear account of the key features social workers need to bear in mind when reviewing their assessments or interventions. In judging how much more or less probable a theory or hypothesis is in the light of new evidence, the main variables to remember are how probable that evidence was even if you did not hold the theory and how strongly the theory predicted that the evidence would be found.

A crucial lesson from science is the reminder that we cannot prove our beliefs beyond all doubt. We can find more or less convincing evidence for a particular assessment of a client but social workers should not forget that they are fallible. Accepting fallibility is rational but can be painful. Social workers may reach their judgements with only a degree of confidence but they cannot act by degrees; they have to take decisive actions. They have, for example, either to remove a child or leave him at home. It would, in some ways, be easier to carry out such decisions confident that the actions were absolutely in the best interests of the child. Unfortunately, we are not justified in having such confidence. We can only be confident that we are making the 'right' decision in the sense that it is the best on the available evidence, not that it is right in the sense of being certainly true.

The public's anger and criticism of social workers and other professionals, in recent years, has been fuelled by practitioners' apparent over-confidence in their judgements. This was, for example, a significant factor in coverage of the events in Cleveland in 1987. There was a dramatic rise in the number of diagnoses of child sexual abuse by two paediatricians. In five months in 1987, mainly in just two months, sexual abuse was diagnosed in one hundred and twenty-one children, all of whom were then removed from their parents while further investigations were made. Because of the public outcry, an inquiry was set up by the government. This inquiry found that the paediatricians had unreasonable confidence in the 'anal dilatation test' as a means of diagnosing abuse. A positive result was seen not as 'grounds of strong suspicion' but as 'an unequivocal "diagnosis" of sexual abuse' (HMSO, 1988, p. 243). The senior social worker with main responsibility for organising the social work response was criticised for a similar over-confidence: 'the possibility of misdiagnosis had not occurred to her' (HMSO, 1988, p. 82). This confidence in the test results influenced all their subsequent actions.

This was particularly apparent in the way they responded to criticisms. The police were the first to show doubt and ask for further evidence to confirm the allegation of abuse, partly to help them identify and prose-

cute the offender and partly because the police surgeon,
like many other doctors, considered the dilatation test
was suggestive but far from diagnostic of abuse. The
paediatricians and social workers rejected the concerns of
the police surgeon and excluded her from the investigations. Indeed the Director of Social Services went so
far as to send a memo to all social workers which 'directed
the exclusion of police surgeons from examining children
referred to social services for reasons of sexual abuse'
(HMSO, 1988, p. 65).

The failure to doubt the accuracy of the test was also
apparent in the 'disclosure work' that the social workers
did with the children. The purpose of these interviews is
to investigate a suspicion of abuse, using play materials to
make it easier for the children to express themselves. The
inquiry found that the social workers 'worked from the
presumption that the children had been abused (HMSO,
1988, p. 59). Denial of abuse was interpreted as a psychological process of blocking out a traumatic experience, to
be overcome by asking leading questions. No serious
consideration was given to the possibility that, when a
child denied being abused, he or she was speaking the
truth. The Cleveland Report complains that: 'those conducting the interviews seemed unaware of the extent of
pressure, even coercion, in their approach' (HMSO, 1988,
p. 209). Over-confidence can have painful consequences
for social workers' clients.

Where previous advocates of science tended to present
social workers with a sharp dichotomy of scientific/
unscientific, acceptable/ unacceptable, scientific methods
now are presented as a continuum. Positivists asserted
that only behavioural terms were acceptable; empiricists
consider psychological terms can be rendered reliable and
valid. Positivists tended to devalue empathy and intuition
as inferior to scientific reasoning and some saw empathy
in particular as a nuisance, interfering with researchers'

ability to study people objectively. Empiricists think empathy is a valuable skill while intuitive reasoning can never be wholly eradicated. With both, their limitations need to be remembered and compensated for as much as possible. Many positivists claimed that random trials were the only way any causal inferences could be made; a single case permitted no conclusions about causal links to be drawn (e.g. Shyne, 1963). To empiricists, single cases can increase the probability of an hypothesis, depending on what is known about the natural history of that type of problem. Viewing scientific methods in this way offers a far more feasible project to social workers, allowing them to try to use scientific standards of reasoning as much as is possible, given the constraints and pressures of daily practice.

The reality of social workers' work conditions are important. Although the discussion has focused on how the practitioner could use scientific methods, it is not realistic to expect individual social workers to take sole responsibility for changing the way they work. The profession in general needs to accept the challenge of being more rigorous and critical about their reasoning. Change has repercussions for social work training, management, and supervision. Social workers need time, help and encouragement from their seniors to adopt new standards. Heavy caseloads, stressful deadlines, and poor supervision are common experiences for social workers today, all acting against the drive for higher standards of practice.

What can we hope to achieve by adopting scientific methods in social work? The advocates of science have always seen its chief merit as being that it offers the hope of developing effective ways of helping clients. This must be balanced by the recognition that human behaviour and the social world are complex phenomena that are unlikely to yield easily to detailed understanding. The possibility of developing general theories explaining human actions with precision seems remote. Reamer, an American academic, advises cautious expectations:

> It is unlikely we will ever be in a position to make sweeping theoretical statements about the etiology of social problems, effective interventions, and so on. Far more likely is that our aim will be toward what Merton (1949) dubbed 'theories of the middle range', that is midlevel theories whose main purpose is to help practitioners understand discrete aspects of social problems and interventions relevant to them. (1993, p. 152)

This book does not and cannot contain simple instructions on how to develop social work's knowledge base. There are no mechanical rules for developing theories, for clarifying concepts so that they have a clear, shared meaning, for reaching a consensus on which theory is most probable, nor for dealing with the complex web of moral, economic and empirical factors relevant to making practical decisions in social work. Intelligence, imagination, and hard work are needed. Nor will these efforts produce a body of certain truths. Adopting scientific standards of reasoning will make social workers more aware of their fallibility. The psychological feeling of certainty that intuitive understanding can create will be recognised as having only a tenuous link to justified confidence. If the process is hard and the result is imperfect, one could question whether it is worth the effort. The justification lies in the importance of social work as a means of reducing human misery. Scientific methods of reasoning hold no guarantee of success but offer the best hope of achieving this goal effectively.

Bibliography

Area Review Committee (1989) *The Doreen Aston Report.* London: London Borough of Lambeth.

Ayer, A.J. (1976) *The Central Questions of Philosophy*, London Penguin Books.

Bacon, F. (1620) *The New Organon and Related Writings.* Published, 1960, New York: Liberal Arts Press.

Berkowitz, R *et al* (1981) 'Lowering expressed emotion in relatives of schizophrenics'. In Goldstein, M. (ed.) *New Developments in Interventions with Families of Schizophrenics*, Jessey-Bass, San Francisco

Birmingham City Council (1981) *Joint enquiry arising from the death of Neil Howlett*, Birmingham: Birmingham City Council.

Booth, C. (1889) *Life and Labour of the People of London,* vol. 1 London, Macmillan.

Brewer, C. and Lait, J. (1980) *Can Social Work Survive?* London: Temple Smith.

Bridgeman, P. (1927) *The Logic of Modern Physics*, New York: Macmillan.

Brown, G. and Birley, J. (1968) 'Crises and life changes and the onset of schizophrenia'. *Journal of Health and Social Behaviour*, Volume 9 203–214.

Brown, G. and Harris, T. (1978) *Social Origins of Depression*, London: Tavistock.

Brown, G., Monck, E., Carstairs, G. and Wing, J. (1962) 'Influence of family life on the course of schizophrenic disorders' *British Journal of Preventive and Social Medicine*, Volume 16 55–68.

Brown, G. and Rutter, M. (1966) 'The measurement of family

activities and relationships: A methodological study' *Human Relations*, Volume 19.

Brown, G. and Wing, J (1972) 'Influence of family life on the course of schizophrenic disorders: a replication' *British Journal of Psychiatry*, Volume 121 241.

Browne, K., Davies, C. and Stratton, P. (eds) (1989) *Early Prediction and Prevention of Child Abuse*, Chichester: Wiley.

Browne, K. and Saqi, S. (1989) 'Approaches to Screening for Child Abuse and Neglect.' In Browne K. *et al* (eds) *Early Prediction and Prevention of Child Abuse*. Chichester: Wiley.

Byrne, T. and Padfield, C. (1990) *Social Services*, Heinemann, London, Made Simple Books.

Carew, R. (1979) 'The Place of Knowledge in Social Work Activity'. *British Journal of Social Work*, vol.9, no.3 349–364.

Carnap, R. (1953) 'Testability and Meaning'. In Feigh, H. and Brodbeck, M. (eds) *Readings in the Philosophy of Science*, New York: Appleton-Century-Crofts.

Carnap, R. (1975) 'Psychological Terms can all be Reduced to Observable Thing-Predicates'. In Krimmerman, L. (ed.) *The Nature and Scope of Social Science: A Critical Anthology*, New York: Appleton-Century-Crofts.

Cassons P. (1982) *Social Work Courses*, London: CCETSW Study 5.

CCETSW (1989) *Statement of Requirements for Qualification in Social Work*, London: CCETSW.

CCETSW (1995) *Paper 30, Revised edition: Rules and Requirements for the Diploma in Social Work*, London: CCETSW.

Charities Organisation Society (1890) *Form no. 28, Notice to persons Applying for Assistance*. In 'C.O.S. Forms, Papers, Investigating Tickets, Byelaws Almanak etc 1877–90' in the possession of the Family Welfare Association (formerly COS) Denison House, London.

Clwyd Report (1996), Clwyd County Council.

Collingwood, R. (1946) *The Idea of History*, Oxford, Oxford University Press.

Cope Report (1951) *Report of the Committee on Medical Auxiliaries*, Cmnd 8188, London, HMSO.

Corby B. (1982) 'Theory and Practice in Long Term Social Work' *British Journal of Social Work*, 12, no. 6 pp. 619–638.

Corrigan, P. and Leonard, P. (1978) *Social Work Practice Under Capitalism*, London: Macmillan.

Curnock, K. and Hardiker, P. (1979) *Towards Practice Theory: Skills and methods in social assessments*, London: R.K.P.

Dana, B. (1965) 'Enriching Social Work Education with Mental

204

Retardation Content' *Journal of Education for Social Work*, vol. 1, no.2.

Davies, M. (1974) 'The Current Status of Social Work research'. *British Journal of Social Work*, vol.4, no. 3 pp. 281–303.

Dennett, D. (1984) *Elbow Room*. Oxford: Clarendon Press.

DHSS (1981) *Social Work: A Research Review*, HMSO Research Report no.8 London: HMSO.

Department of Health (1988) *Protecting Children: A Guide for Social Workers undertaking a Comprehensive Assessment*. London: HMSO.

Department of Health (1991) *Working Together: A guide to arrangements for interagency co-operation for the protection of children from abuse*, London, HMSO.

Dingwall, R. (1986) 'The Jasmine Beckford Affair'. *Modern Law Review*, vol. 49, no.4, pp. 489–507.

Dorling, J. (1979) 'Bayesian Personalism, the Methodology of Research programmes and Duhem's Problem', *Studies in History and Philosophy of Science*, vol.10 177–187.

Downie, R. and Telfer, E. (1980) *Caring and Curing*, London: Methuen.

Duhem, P. (1905) *The Aim and Structure of Physical Theory*, Princeton: Princeton University Press.

Elks, M. and Kirkhart, K. (1993) 'Evaluating Effectiveness from the Practitioner Perspective'. *Social Work,* Volume 38, Number 5, pp. 554–563.

Ellwood, C. (1918) *Social Facts and Scientific Social Work*, Proceedings of the National Conference of Social Work.

England, H. (1986) *Social Work as Art*, London: Allen and Unwin.

Essex County Council and Essex Area Health Authority (1981) Malcolm Page. Essex County Council.

Everitt, A., Hardiker, P., Littlewood, J. and Mullender, A. (1992) *Applied Research for Better Practice*, London: Macmillan.

Eysenck, H. (1986) *Decline and Fall of the Freudian Empire*, London: Pelican Books.

Farrell, B.A. (1981) *The Standing of Psychoanalysis*, Oxford: Oxford University Press.

Fischer, J. (1973) 'Is Casework Effective? A Review'. *Social Work*, May, vol. 1 pp. 5–20.

Fischer, J (1976) *The Effectiveness of Social Casework*, Springfield, Charles Thomas.

Freud, S. (1912) *Recommendations for physicians on the psycho-analytic method for treatment*, Standard Edition, 12, London: Hogarth Press.

Fuller, R. and Petch, A. (1995) *Practitioner Research: the Reflexive Social Worker*. Buckingham: Open University Press.

Gambrill, E. (1990) *Critical Thinking in Clinical Practice*. San Francisco: Jossey-Bass.

Garfield, S. and Bergin, A. (1978) *Handbook of Psychotherapy Change*, New York: Wiley.

Giedymin, J. (1975) 'Antipositivism in Contemporary Philosophy of Social Science and Humanities' *British Journal for the Philosophy of Science*, vol. 26.

Goldberg, M. and Warburton, R. (1979) *Ends and Means in Social Work*, London: George Allen and Unwin.

Goldstein, H. (1973) *Social Work Practice: A Unitary Approach*, University of South Carolina Press.

Goldstein, H. (1986) 'Towards the Integration of Theory and Practice: A Humanistic Approach'. *Social Work*, Sept–Oct 352–357.

Glover, E. (1955) *The Technique of Psycho-Analysis*, New York: International Universities Press.

Hadley, R. and Clough, R. (1996) *Care in Chaos: Frustration and Challenge in Community Care*, London, Cassell.

Hardiker, P. (1981) 'Heart and Head – The Function and Role of Knowledge in Social Work'. *Issues in Social Work Education*, vol. 1, no.2, pp. 85–111.

Hardiker, P. and Webb, D. (1970) 'Explaining deviant behaviour: the social context of "action" and "infraction" accounts in the probation service'. *Sociology*, vol. 13, no.1, pp. 1–17.

Hawton, K (ed.) (1989) *Cognitive-Behavioural Therapy for Psychiatric Problems: A Practical Guide*, Oxford, Oxford University Press.

Heineman M. (1981) 'The Obsolete Scientific Imperative in Social Work Research' *Social Service Review*, Sept, pp. 371–397.

Hempel, C. (1966) 'Recent Problems of Induction'. In Colodney, R. (ed.) *Mind and Cosmos*. Pittsburgh, University of Pittsburgh.

HMSO (1974) *Report of the Committee of Inquiry into the Care and Supervision Provided in Relation to Maria Colwell*, London: HMSO.

HMSO (1975a) *Report of the Committee of Inquiry into the Consideration given and steps taken towards securing the welfare of Richard Clark by Perth Town Council and other bodies or persons concerned*, Edinburgh: HMSO.

HMSO (1975b) *The Report of the Committee of Inquiry into the provision and co-ordination of services to the family of John George Aukland*, London: HMSO.

HMSO (1980) *The Report of the Committee of Inquiry into the case of Paul Steven Brown*, London: HMSO.

HMSO (1988) *Report of the Inquiry into Child Abuse in Cleveland 1987*, London: HMSO.

HMSO (1992) *The Report of the Inquiry into the Removal of Children from Orkney in February 1991*, Edinburgh: HMSO.

Hobbes, T. (1651) *Leviathan* Ed. Michael Oakeshott, Oxford. Blackwell (1966 ed).

Hollis, F. (1966) *Casework: A Psychosocial Therapy*, New York: Random House.

Howe, D. (1987) *An Introduction to Social Work Theory*, Aldershot, Wildwood House.

Howe D. (1994) 'Modernity, Postmodernity and Social Work'. *British Journal of Social Work*, vol. 24 pp. 513–532.

Howson, C. and Urbach, P. (1989) *Scientific Reasoning: the Bayesian Approach*, Illinois: Open Court.

Hudson, B. and McDonald, G. (1986) *Behavioural Social Work: An Introduction*, London: Macmillan.

Hume, D. (1739) *A Treatise on Human Nature*, edited by Selbey-Bigge (1964), Oxford: Clarendon Press.

Jehu, D. (1967) *Learning Theory and Social Work*, London: Routledge and Kegan Paul.

Jordan, B. (1979) *Helping in Social Work*, London: Routledge and Kegan Paul.

Kahneman, D., Slovic, P, and Tversky, A. (eds) (1990) *Judgement under uncertainty: Heuristics and biases*, Cambridge: Cambridge University Press.

Karpf, M. (1931) *The Scientific Basis of Social Work*, New York: Columbia University Press.

Kilbrandon Report, (1964) *Report of the Committee on Children and Young Persons (Scotland)*, Edinburgh: HMSO.

Kirk, S. (1979) 'Understanding Research Utilization in Social Work'. In Rubin, A. and Rosenblatt, A. (eds.) *Sourcebook on Research Utilization*, New York: Council on Social Work Education.

Krimmerman, L. (ed.) (1975) *The Nature and Scope of Social science: A Critical Anthology*, New York: Appleton-Century-Crofts.

Kuhn, T. (1970) *The Structure of Scientific Revolutions*, Chicago: University of Chicago Press, 2nd ed.

Kuhn, T. (1976) 'Theory-Change as Structure-Change: Comments on the Sneed Formalism', *Erkenntnis*, 10, pp. 179–99.

Kuhn, T. (1978) *The Essential Tension*, Chicago: University of Chicago Press.

Lakatos, I. (1978) *Philosophical Papers*, vol. 2. edited by J. Worrall and G. Currie, Cambridge: Cambridge University Press.

Lakatos, I. and Musgrave, A. (eds) (1970) *Criticism and the Growth of Knowledge*, Cambridge: Cambridge University Press.

Levy, A. and Kahan, B. (1991) *The Pindown Experience and the Protection of Children: Report of the Staffordshire Child Care Inquiry, 1990*, Stafford: Staffordshire County Council.

Loewenberg, F. (1984) 'Professional Ideology, Middle Range Theories, and Knowledge Building for Social Work Practice'. *British Journal of Social Work*, 14, pp. 309–322.

London Borough of Bexley (1982) *Report of the Panel of Inquiry with reference to Linda Gates and her family*, London Borough of Bexley.

London Borough of Brent (1985) *A Child in Trust*, London Borough of Brent.

London Borough of Greenwich (1987) *A Child in Mind: Protection of Children in a Responsible Society*, London Borough of Greenwich.

London Borough of Lambeth (1987) *Whose Child? The Report of the Public Inquiry into the death of Tyra Henry*, London Borough of Lambeth.

Mater, J.E. and Timms, N. (1970) *The Client Speaks*, London: Routledge and Kegan Paul.

McDonald, G. (1994) 'Developing Empirically-Based Practice in Probation'. *British Journal of Social Work*, vol. 24, 405–427.

McDonald, G. and Sheldon, B. (1992) 'Contemporary Studies of the Effectiveness of Social Work'. *British Journal of Social Work*, vol. 22, no. 6, pp. 615–643.

Mandler, J and Mandler, G. (1964) *Thinking: From Association to Gestalt*, New York: Wiley.

Mill, J.S. (1867) *An Examination of Sir William Hamilton's Philosophy*, London: Longman.

Mitchell, K. *et al* (1973) 'Antecedents to Therapeutic Outcome'. *NIMH Grant Report (12306)*, University of Arkansas/Arkansas Rehabilitation Services.

Mitchell, K. *et al* (1977) 'A reappraisal of the therapeutic effectiveness of accurate empathy, nonpossessive warmth, and genuineness'. In Gurman, A.S. and Razin, A.M. (eds) *Effective Psychotherapy: A Handbook of Research*, New York: Pergamon Press.

Mullen, E.J. and Dumpson, J.R. (1972) *Evaluation of Social Intervention*, San Francisco, Jossey Bass.

Munro, E. (1994) 'Not Guilty' *Community Care*, 14th July, p. 29.

Munro, E. (1996) 'Avoidable and Unavoidable Mistakes in Child

Protection Work'. *British Journal of Social Work*, vol. 26, no. 6, pp. 793–808.

Munro, E. (1997) 'Improving Social Workers' Knowledge Base in Child Protection Work'. *British Journal of Social Work*, vol. 27, no. 6 (in press).

Nagel, E. (1961) *The Structure of Science*, London: Routledge and Kegan Paul.

Newton-Smith, W.H. (1981) *The Rationality of Science*, London: Routledge and Kegan Paul.

Nisbett, R. and Ross, L. (1980) *Human Inference: strategies and shortcomings of social judgement*, New Jersey, Prentice-Hall.

Northern Regional Health Authority (1989) *Report of the Independent Inquiry Team's Review of the Care of Karl John McGoldrick*, Newcastle, Northern Regional Health Authority.

Nottinghamshire Area Child Protection Committee (1994) *Report of Overview Group into the Circumstances Surrounding the Death of Leanne White*, Nottingham: Nottinghamshire County Council.

O'Connor, D. (1971) *Free Will*, London: Macmillan.

O'Hear, A. (1989) *An Introduction to the Philosophy of Science*, Oxford: Clarendon Press.

Orcutt, B. (1990) *Science and Inquiry in Social Work Practice*, New York: Columbia University Press.

Paley, J. (1987) 'Social Work and the Sociology of Knowledge'. *British Journal of Social Work*, vol.17, pp. 169–186.

Papineau, D. (1978) *For Science in the Social Sciences*, London: Macmillan.

Pardeck, J., Murphy, J. and Choi, J.M. (1994) 'Some implications of postmodernism for social work practice'. *Social Work*, vol. 39, no. 4, pp 343–6.

Parsloe, P. and Stevenson, O. (1978) *Social Service Teams: The Practitioners' View*, London: DHSS.

Parton, N. (1994) 'Problematics of Government, (Post) Modernity and Social Work'. *British Journal of Social Work*, vol. 24, no.1, pp. 9–32.

Payne, M. (1991) *Modern Social Work Theory: A Critical Introduction*, London: Macmillan.

Pearson, G., Treseder, J., and Yellolly, M. (1988) *Social Work and the Legacy of Freud*, London: Macmillan.

Perlman, H. (1965) 'Self-determination: reality or illusion?' *Social Service Review*. vol. 39, no. 4 pp. 410–421.

Philp, M. (1979) 'Notes on the Form of Knowledge in Social Work'. *Sociological Review*, vol. 27, no. 1, pp. 83–111.

Polanyi, M. (1967) *The Tacit Dimension*, New York: Garden City.

Popper, K. (1959) *The Logic of Scientific Discovery*, London: Hutchison.

Popper, K. (1963) *Conjectures and Refutations*, London: Routledge and Kegan Paul.

Pozatek, E. (1994) 'The problem of certainty: clinical social work in the postmodern era'. *Social Work*, vol. 39, no. 4, pp. 396–403.

Putnam, H. (1978) *Meaning and the Moral Sciences*. London: Routledge and Kegan Paul.

Putnam, H. (1974) 'The "corroboration" of theories' In Schilpp, P.A. (ed.) *The Philosophy of Karl Popper*, vol.2, La Salle, Illinois: Open Court.

Putnam, H. (1981) *Reason Truth and History*, Cambridge: Cambridge University Press.

Putnam, H. (1992) *Realism with a Human Face*, Massachusetts: Harvard University Press.

Quine, W.V.O.(1953) *From a Logical Point of View*, Cambridge Mass, Harvard University Press.

Ragg, N. (1977) *People Not Cases: A Philosophical Approach to Social Work*, London: Routledge and Kegan Paul.

Randall, F. (1981) *British Social Services*, London: Macdonald and Evans.

Raynor, P. (1984) 'Evaluation with One Eye Closed: The Empiricist Agenda in Social Work Research', *British Journal of Social Work*, vol. 4, pp. 1–10.

Reamer, F. (1993) *The Philosophical Foundations of Social Work*, New York: Columbia University Press.

Reid, W. (1994) 'The Empirical Practice Movement' *Social Service Review,* June.

Reid, W. and Hanrahan, P. The Effectiveness of Social Work, Recent Evidence (1980). In Goldberg, E. and Warburton, R. (eds.) *Ends and Means in Social Work*, London, George Allen and Unwin.

Reid, W. and Smith, A. (1989) *Research in Social Work*, New York: Columbia University Press.

Richmond, M. (1899) 'The Settlement and Friendly Visiting' in Colcord, J. and Mann, R. *The Long View: Papers and Addresses by Mary E. Richmond,* New York: Russell Sage Foundation.

Richmond, M. (1917) *Social Diagnosis*, New York: Russell Sage Foundation.

Rogers, C. (1957) 'The Necessary and Sufficient Conditions of Therapeutic Personality Change' *Journal of Consulting Psychology*, vol. 21, pp. 95–103.

Rogers, C. (1961) *On Becoming a Person*, London: Constable.

Rorty, R. (1979) *Philosophy and the Mirror of Nature*. Oxford, Blackwells.

Rorty, R. (1991) *Objectivity, Relativism and Truth*, Cambridge, Cambridge: University Press.

Rosenberg, A. (1988) *Philosophy of Social Science*, Cambridge: Clarendon Press.

Rosenblatt, A. (1968) 'The Practitioner's Use and Evaluation of Research'. *Social Work*, vol.13, no.1, pp. 53–9.

Rowntree Seebohm (1902) *Poverty: A Study of Town Life*, London: Macmillan.

Ruchdeschel, R. and Farris, B. (1982) 'Science: Critical Faith or Dogmatic Ritual?' *Social Casework*, May, pp. 272–275.

Russell, B. (1927) *Philosophy*, New York: Norton.

Rutter, M. and Brown, G. (1966) 'The reliability and validity of measures of family life and relationships in families containing a psychiatric patient'. *Social Psychiatry*, Volume 1, pp. 38–53.

Sainsbury, E. (1975) *Social Work with Families: Perceptions of Social Casework among Clients of a Family Service Unit*, London Routledge and Kegan Paul.

Secker, J. (1993) *From Theory to Practice in Social Work*. Aldershot: Avebury.

Seebohm, F. (1968) *Report on the Local Authority and Allied Personal Social Services*, London: HMSO.

Segal, S. (1972) 'Research on the outcomes of social work therapeutic interventions: a review of the literature'. *Journal of Health and Social Behaviour*, 13, pp. 3–17.

Shaw, I. and Walton R. (1978) 'Education for Practice: former students' attitudes to a social work course'. *Contemporary Social Work Education*, vol.2, no.1, pp. 15–20.

Sheldon, B. (1978) 'Theory and Practice in Social Work: a Re-examination of a Tenuous Relationship'. *British Journal of Social Work*, Vol 8, pp.1–22.

Sheldon, B. (1982) 'A Measure of Success', *Social Work Today*, 13, no.21, pp. 8–11.

Sheldon, B. (1986) 'Social Work Effectiveness Experiments: review and implications' *British Journal of Social Work*, vol. 1, pp. 223–242.

Sheldon, B. (1987) 'Implementing Findings from Social Work Effectiveness Research' *British Journal of Social Work*, vol. 17, pp. 573–586.

Shyne, A. (1963) 'Evaluation of Results in Social Work', *Social Work,* October, pp. 26–33.

Skinner, B.F. (1974) *About Behaviourism*, London, Jonathan Cape.

Social Services Inspectorate (1991) *Children in the Public Care: A Review of Residential Child Care*, London: HMSO.

Social Services Inspectorate (1993) *Evaluating Child protection Services: Findings and Issues*, London: Department of Health.

Stevenson, O. (ed.) (1989) *Child Abuse: Public Policy and Professional Practice*, London: Harvester Wheatsheaf.

Strupp, H. (1969) *Patients View Their Psychotherapy*, Baltimore, Johns Hopkins University Press.

Strupp, H., Hadley, S. and Gomes-Schwartz, B. (1977) *Psychotherapy for Better or Worse: The Problem of Negative Effects*, New York: Jason Aronson.

Taylor, C. (1964) *The Explanation of Behaviour*, London: Routledge and Kegan Paul.

Taylor, I. (1993) 'A Case for Social Work Evaluation of Social Work Education'. *British Journal of Social Work,* vol. 23, pp. 123–38.

Thorpe, D. (1994) *Evaluating Child Protection*, Buckingham: Open University Press.

Tripodi, T. (1983) *Evaluative Research for Social Workers*, New Jersey: Prentice-Hall.

Truax, C., Carkhuff, R., and Kodman, F. (1965) 'Relationships between therapist-offered conditions and patient change in group psychotherapy' *Journal of Clinical Psychology*, 21, pp. 327–329.

Truax, C. and Mitchell, K. (1971) 'Research on Certain Therapist Interpersonal Skills in relation to Process and Outcome'. In Bergin, A. and Garfield, S. (eds) *Handbook of Psychotherapy and Behaviour Change*, New York: Wiley.

United Nations Dept of Economic and Social Affairs (1958) *Training for Social Work: Third International Survey*, New York: United Nations.

Urbach, P. (1987) *Francis Bacon's Philosophy of Science*, La Salle, Illinois: Open Court.

Vaughn, C. and Leff, J. (1976) 'The measurement of expressed emotion in families of psychiatric patients'. *British Journal of Social and Clinical Psychology,* Volume 15, pp. 157–165.

Vernon, J. and Fruin, D. (1986) *In Care: A Study of Social Work Decision-Making*, London: National Children's Bureau.

Walker, J., McCarthy, P, Morgan, W., and Timms, N. (1995) *In Pursuit of Quality: Improving Practice Teaching in Social Work*, London: CCETSW.

Wandsworth Area Child Protection Committee (1990) *The Report of the Stephanie Fox Practice Review*, London: London Borough of Wandsworth.

Waterhouse, L. (1987) 'The Relationship between Theory and Practice in Social Work Training'. *Issues in Social Work Education*, 7, no.1.

Watson, J. (1913) 'Psychology as a behaviourist views it'. *Psychological Review,* 20, pp. 158–77.

Watson, J. (1924) *Psychology from the standpoint of a behaviourist*, Philadelphia: Lippincot.

Weick, A. (1987) 'Reconceptualizing the Philosophical Perspective of Social Work'. *Social Service Review*, June, pp. 218–230.

Wilkes, R. (1981) *Social Work with Undervalued Groups*, London: Tavistock.

Wood, K. (1978) 'Casework effectiveness: a new look at the research evidence'. *Social Work*, November, pp. 437–457.

Woodroofe, K. (1962) *From Charity to Social Work in England and the United States*, London: Routlegde and Kegan Paul.

Yellolly, M. (1980) *Social Work Theory and Psychoanalysis*, London: Nostrand Reinhold.

Zurriff, G. (1990) *Behaviourism: A Conceptual Reconstruction*, New York: Columbia University Press.

Index